The Yummy Mummy Kitchen

The Yummy Mummy Kitchen

100 Effortless and Irresistible Recipes to
Nourish Your Family with Style and Grace

MARINA DELIO

HarperOne
An Imprint of HarperCollinsPublishers

Photographs on pages ii, iv, xii (top), 2, 4, 10, 20, 137, 145, 160, 190, 199, 201, 210, 224, and 232 (bottom) © Colleen Riley. All other photographs © Marina Delio.

HarperCollins books may be purchased for educational, business, or sales promotional use. For information please e-mail the Special Markets Department at SPsales@harpercollins.com.

HarperCollins website: http://www.harpercollins.com

HarperCollins®, ™®, and HarperOne™ are trademarks of HarperCollins Publishers.

FIRST EDITION

Designed by Campana Design

Library of Congress Cataloging-in-Publication Data

Delio, Marina.
  The yummy mummy kitchen : 100 effortless and irresist-ible recipes to nourish your family with style and grace / Marina Delio. — 1st ed.
    p. cm.
  ISBN 978–0–06–221355–6
  1. Cooking. I. Title.

TX714.D4425 2013
641.5—dc23

2012023459

13 14 15 16 17 RRD(SC) 10 9 8 7 6 5 4 3 2 1

For my beautiful girls, who bring me so much joy and inspire me to be the best mummy I can be

I owe thanks to many more people than I can even begin to name. I will start with my family, who have always supported me. Thank you especially to the Yummy Mummies in my life who have shaped who I am as a mom. To my own mom, who made homemade dinners every night and showed me the importance of parents' presence in their children's lives. To my parents for making family dinnertime mandatory and instilling an appreciation for healthy eating, and also for sharing some of their delicious recipes. To my grandmother Tai Tai, for passing down some wonderful recipes, traditions, stories, history, and positive attitude. To my husband, Phil, for always supporting and encouraging me throughout the writing of this book—and helping with the dishes after my cooking adventures.

To the girlfriends I am so lucky to have. Laurie, Ronda, Sarah, and Victoria— thank you for always being ready for a mommy happy hour. You are shining examples of glamorous but humble Yummy Mummies and have influenced this book and me in innumerable ways. Thank you to all my many other mommy friends as well.

Thank you to my amazing literary agent, Coleen O'Shea, who knew I could write a beautiful cookbook even before I did, for guiding me through this process and holding my hand from across the country. To my sweet editor, Jeanette Perez at HarperOne, who has been incredibly positive and gently given wonderful suggestions to make this book the best it can be, and the entire team at HarperOne. Also to Colleen Riley Photography for taking the beautiful pictures of the girls and me.

Thank you all so much for making this book possible.

CONTENTS

I'm not the Yummy Mummy. You are. If you don't feel like one now, you surely will after trying some of the easy, wholesome, and delicious recipes from *The Yummy Mummy Kitchen*.

What is a Yummy Mummy? you ask. "Yummy Mummy" is a British term for an attractive, stylish mother. In my definition, however, a Yummy Mummy is a loving and dedicated mom who embodies a healthy lifestyle while retaining a sense of the person she was before having kids. A Yummy Mummy laughs off the spit-up trickling down the back of her shirt and smashed Cheerios at the bottom of her purse. She cooks with the kids even if it means wiping splattered muffin batter off the side of the oven, because that spoon-wielding toddler is having a ball. She holds on to her style and grace even with small children at home and in the most unglamorous of times.

A Yummy Mummy is not a high-maintenance mom. Being a Yummy Mummy does not mean weekly manicures, grocery shopping in stilettos, or nannies. It has nothing to do with money or perfection; it's an attitude. She puts the kids first, but also takes care of herself and finds balance amid the chaos. Putting on a coat of mascara and lip gloss takes just a minute and makes her feel beautiful, or "yummy." Similarly, she knows how to turn a simple meal into a special one with just a little effort. A Yummy Mummy knows that adding a touch of glamour to everything—self, home, meals, and entertaining—makes life more fun and is a special way she can take care of herself and her family.

The Yummy Mummy ideal has been ingrained in me through my British grandmother, the original Yummy Mummy, who is still very chic and has a sparkle in her eye at ninety-two years old. Actually, she says that *her* mom, Val, was the original Yummy Mummy. Having grown up in Hong Kong and Shanghai, my grandmother is called Tai Tai, a term used in parts of Asia to describe the matriarch of a family. She shops at the farmers' market, eats well, and if you meet her, she'll probably say, "Dah-ling, please

come in and have a cocktail!" Having grown up with Yummy Mummies as role models, my own mom became a Yummy Mummy herself. The name of my blog, and this cook-book, is derived from my life as a new mom, trying to be my own version of a good modern mummy while sharing my passion for creating easy recipes that look and taste delicious and make us feel great.

My recipes may look elegant and complicated, but they are deceptively simple. I use as few ingredients as possible, so that the recipes are quick and easy for busy moms like myself to make, even with a toddler on the hip. The secret is that simplic-ity is what makes food taste delicious and look bright and beautiful. Inspired by the foods and produce in my hometown of Santa Barbara and trips to Italy, where I really fell in love with cooking, I have created over a hundred mostly meatless, produce-rich recipes. Getting back to the basics of cooking with fresh seasonal ingredients and making homemade desserts is easy and satisfying. It brings out the Yummy Mummy in all of us.

Feeding our families can feel overwhelming and time-consuming, but I've learned how to simplify meals and get my children involved. Whether I'm throwing ingredients in the slow cooker in the morning, preparing lasagna while my children are napping, or cooking with my daughters in the evening, I love it. Right when my little toddler and preschooler are about to have a meltdown and start the five o'clock whinies, I blast silly music in the kitchen, and the three of us rock out while we cook.

I don't care how ridiculous we look. The three of us are having fun, a healthy dinner is being made, and the kids have no idea how much they are learning. I love the way the colors of fresh produce enhance each other; the popping, sizzling, crunching sounds; the intoxicating smells that fill our home; the wave of heat upon opening the oven; the taste of the dinner coming together on a wooden spoon. It makes me feel happy to make a batch of muffins with my girls and see them sitting on a pretty cake stand on the counter. It makes me proud to hear my kids say, "Mommy, this is the best dinner ever!" I hope *The Yummy Mummy Kitchen* shows you that dinnertime can be not only easy and stress-free, but a time to relish, to create, to bond with family, and to feel good about yourself. Modern moms can be both Mummy and Yummy, and it doesn't have to be hard or time-consuming.

As a former elementary-school teacher observing eating habits and now as a mom noticing restaurant kids' menus devoid of vegetables, I understand how important it is that we teach our kids to respect food. In this book I ask you not to hide pureed vegetables in your children's meals, but to celebrate them, so that our kids will grow up with a palate and an attitude that appreciate foods in their natural form rather than in the overprocessed form many have grown accustomed to. (See "Eat Your Veggies First: Tips for Getting Kids to Eat and Enjoy Vegetables," page 229.) This cookbook is filled with recipes and tips for creating healthy meals in less time than it would take to go out for fast food and with any seasonal produce you happen to have on hand.

Many of my dinner recipes are just one dish or can be made in advance. Easy Greens and Goat Cheese Lasagna (page 138) is a snap to make using store-bought pesto sauce; it is a one-dish meal that can be made up to a day in advance or frozen. With its cheesy topping, even kids who claim not to like vegetables gobble

this lasagna up. My "fancy" appetizers are actually very simple and can be made ahead of time. My Sparkling Cranberry and Brie Bites (page 18) can be prepped up to three days in advance and assembled later. Both picky children and discriminating adults love the sweet taste and glittering appeal of this recipe and don't believe it takes only 10 minutes of active cooking time.

The Yummy Mummy Kitchen shows busy moms how to easily make wholesome dishes that all ages will enjoy. A lifelong lover of fresh produce, I've found the most healthful and delicious ways to cook with fresh fruits and vegetables. Kids often cringe at a mound of soggy vegetables on the side of the plate. However, fresh spinach leaves wilted into pasta, quiche, and enchiladas are rarely picked out and are actually enjoyed. Kids are attracted to many of these recipes because of their presentation. I like to stuff

sautéed vegetables and lentils into small portobello mushrooms (Lentil Stuffed Porto-bello Mushrooms, page 140), so that they are just the right size for tiny hands. Topped with Parmesan they are almost like little pizzas. Similarly, spaghetti squash served in the squash (Baked Spaghetti Squash and "Meatballs," page 135) and apple salads served in apple bowls (Apple, Pomegranate, and Avocado Salad in Apple Bowls, page 75) are fun and nutritious dishes for kids. Kids like to have choices, so I serve many dishes with toppings that allow kids to customize their dinner. My girls love sprinkling shredded coconut, sliced bananas, raisins, and peanuts over my family's hundred-year-old recipe for curry (Chicken Curry McCutcheon, page 282).

In this book you will find a few of the best-loved recipes from my blog, www .yummymummykitchen.com, some of which have been rewritten or improved. Most of the recipes, however, are new ones I have had fun creating for you over the last few months. Many are recipes I grew up eating and now make for my family with some small changes that allow for even more vegetables at dinner. I hope the recipes on the following pages will give you the confidence to whip up the perfect dish for any occasion, whether it's stylish hors d'oeuvres for a mommy and baby happy-hour play date, a quick family dinner at home, or a stunning dessert. Most important, I hope the recipes make cooking fun and make you feel good—like the Yummy Mummy you truly are.

appetizers, hors d'oeuvres, and snacks

Mini Apple Cheddar Grilled Cheese Sandwiches

Cheddar Herb Shortbread Crackers

Cheesy Broccoli Brown Rice Poppers

Sparkling Cranberry and Brie Bites

Sugared Blueberry Goat Cheese Crostini

Effortless Edamame-Basil Hummus Dip

Eggplant "Fries"

Baked Spinach and Artichoke Dip

Grape and Rosemary Flatbread

Heirloom Tomato and Asiago Tartlets

Peach and Gorgonzola Phyllo Purses

Pear, Humboldt Fog Cheese, and Honey Crisps

Quick Grilled Shrimp in Avocado Boats

Raspberry Endives with Candied Pecans

Balsamic Strawberry Bruschetta

FRIENDSHIP NIBBLES

Every Friday afternoon at four o'clock four of my girlfriends and I get together for a play date with our kids. We call it Mommy Happy Hour. The five of us have been getting together since our first babies were only days old. Our kids have been lucky to have automatic friends they have seen weekly from infancy. They are close in a way that is stronger than typical preschool friendships. However, I'm not sure if it's the kids or the moms who benefit most from weekly happy-hour play dates.

We were blessed to come into each other's lives through an amazing nonprofit organization called Postpartum Education for Parents, or PEP, which hosts new-parent groups, among other services, for new moms and dads. PEP promoted our group as a place to share the "highs and lows" of parenting a newborn and make friendships that last a lifetime. When I attended my first meeting, I had no idea just how much I needed supportive moms with babies the same age in my life. From dealing with breast-feeding issues and commiserating over lack of sleep, to sharing a glass of wine and hors d'oeuvres at the end of the week while our kids played, I realized mommy friends are essential. We are there for each other when life is hard and provide much needed friendship and support from an understanding place. Moms and dads need peers they can relate to, to laugh, cry, and celebrate right alongside them.

I've heard it said that we must "mother the mother." In order for us to be good moms, we must first meet our own needs. It's like emergency oxygen on an airplane. A woman can't give it to her child until she puts her own mask on and can breathe herself first. These Friday happy-hour play dates rejuvenate us and help us to be kinder, more patient moms. The women and I alternate hosting and always set out delectable bite-size snacks. They are simple, easy hors d'oeuvres, and we are always excited to taste new ones (and old favorites) while we chat away about our week. The cute little nibbles make our Friday afternoon ritual even more special than it already is. We raise a glass of our favorite wine and say cheers to all the good things in our lives, while our kids play and snack nearby. Sharing the highs and lows of parenting with good friends over appetizers is something I recommend every parent do on a regular basis. It could be a weekly or monthly play group, a book club, a dinner club, or a happy hour. Yummy Mummies need to find time to support each other.

Appetizers are the food of parties and gatherings. Their small size makes them seem sophisticated, but at the same time carefree. They can be eaten with fingers while standing outside by the sandbox, sitting on the playroom floor, or chatting at a chic cocktail party. Though we may not go out at night as much now that we are moms, we can still have that fun camaraderie over delectable treats in a relaxed setting. What's more, we can share it with our kids, as they get excited about fun snacks and tea-party foods with their friends. I try to make appetizers that are fun, pretty, delicious, and healthy for both adults and kids. When I'm hosting a happy hour or an out-of-town guest stops by unexpectedly, I like to have something special and simple to prepare. Having small bites of appetizers, hors d'oeuvres, and snacks is my favorite way to unwind and catch up with friends from two to ninety-two years old. They make guests feel comfortable and taken care of, and they make the mood more fun. The days of expensive restaurant happy hours are over. Armed with a few simple stylish appetizer recipes, you will find that entertaining can be an effortless and stress-free time to connect with friends and family.

This recipe does double duty, working as a party appetizer or an after-school snack. In our house we even like this for dinner served with a cup of tomato soup or a salad. Apples and fig jam add an irresistible sweetness and elegance to this kid favorite.

Mini Apple Cheddar Grilled Cheese Sandwiches

1 baguette, cut crosswise into ¼-inch slices

3 tablespoons fig jam

2 apples, cored and thinly sliced crosswise and then in half
    to make half-rounds

5 ounces sharp white cheddar cheese, sliced

2 tablespoons butter

1 small bunch fresh rosemary, cut into 3-inch pieces, for
    garnish (optional)

I love serving casual comfort-food appetizers at cocktail parties, happy hours, and book-club meetings. They make guests feel at home.

To assemble the sandwiches, on half of the bread slices spread a thin layer of jam. On each, place a slice of apple and then a slice of cheese. Top with remaining pieces of bread.

Heat the butter in a skillet over medium heat. Cook the sandwiches until the cheese has melted and the bread is golden brown, about 3 minutes per side. Poke the rosemary pieces through the tops of the sandwiches like a skewer, if using.

Makes about 15 mini sandwiches

Keep a log of this cracker dough in the freezer. When guests stop by unexpectedly, you can slice these, pop them in the oven, and have a homemade snack in minutes.

Kids love cheddar crackers. Here they are given an elegant makeover with herbs and sea salt. These crackers are unbelievably easy to make and free of the preservatives found in some processed store-bought crackers. Serve with fresh grapes, dried fruit, and nuts.

Cheddar Herb Shortbread Crackers

½ cup butter, at room temperature

1 cup all-purpose flour

½ cup grated extra-sharp white cheddar cheese

1 teaspoon fresh thyme leaves

¼ teaspoon lavender (optional)

1 teaspoon fleur de sel or coarse sea salt

In a medium bowl, using your hands or a fork, combine the butter with the flour, cheese, thyme, and lavender until it's the consistency of dough. On a piece of plastic wrap, form the dough into a log approximately 2 inches in diameter. Wrap tightly in the plastic wrap. Chill overnight or at least 2 hours.

Preheat the oven to 350°F. Line a cookie sheet with parchment paper. Unwrap the log and cut it into ¼-inch slices. Arrange the slices on the prepared cookie sheet. Lightly sprinkle the slices with salt. Bake for 12 to 15 minutes, until light golden in color. Cool completely.

Makes about 35 (2-inch) crackers

Culinary lavender can be found in the spice section of specialty food stores such as Williams-Sonoma.

Broccoli and cheddar are an irresistible combination. Here the two are baked into healthy and hearty brown rice poppers—a perfect afternoon snack for little hands.

Cheesy Broccoli Brown Rice Poppers

1 cup broccoli florets
2 cups cooked brown rice
2 large eggs, lightly beaten
1 cup grated extra-sharp cheddar cheese
1 tablespoon fresh chopped parsley, plus more for garnish (optional)
½ teaspoon salt
¼ teaspoon freshly cracked pepper
½ cup ¼-inch-diced extra-sharp cheddar cheese

Preheat the oven to 400°F. Generously coat a mini muffin pan with cooking spray.

Heat a saucepan with 1 inch of water and a steamer basket over medium-high heat. Add the broccoli, cover, and steam until tender-crisp, about 3 minutes. Remove and dry the broccoli on paper towels. Cut the broccoli into about 1 teaspoon-size pieces.

In a medium bowl, stir together the rice, eggs, grated cheese, parsley, salt, and pepper. Place 1 teaspoon of the rice mixture at the bottom of each muffin cup until half of the mixture has been used up. Place a small broccoli piece and one cheese cube on top of the rice. Cover the broccoli and cheddar with another teaspoon of the rice mixture. Using your fingers, press the rice mixture to cover the broccoli. Bake for 10 minutes, until the rice has set. Serve warm. Garnish with parsley, if desired.

Makes about 15 to 20 poppers

LIFE TIP

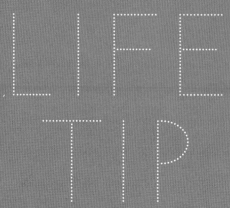

Do you remember having after-school snacks when you were little? I remember feeling so happy and content eating the special treats my mom would make for my friends and me after school. My favorites were grilled cheese sandwiches cut into little houses and chocolate chip cookies. Simple homemade after-school snacks can create these happy memories in your kids and keep hunger pangs away until dinnertime.

Sugared cranberries are easy to make and are very impressive. Fresh cranberries are only available around November and December. For an equally tasty and stunning snack at other times of the year, try the Sugared Blueberry Goat Cheese Crostini on page 22 and bookmark this one for the holidays.

Sparkling Cranberry and Brie Bites

2 cups fresh cranberries

1 cup good maple syrup

1 cup granulated sugar

16 water crackers (such as Carr's)

8 ounces Brie cheese

½ cup cranberry chutney or cranberry relish

Fresh mint, for garnish

Rinse the cranberries and place in a medium bowl. Heat the syrup in a small saucepan until just warm. Pour over the cranberries. (Make sure the syrup is warm, not hot, or the cranberries may pop.) Gently stir with a spoon to coat all the berries. Cool, cover, and let soak in the refrigerator overnight.

The next day drain the cranberries in a colander. Place the sugar in a large bowl or baking dish. Add half of the cranberries and roll them around until lightly coated in sugar; repeat with the other half. Place on a baking sheet and let dry, about 1 hour.

To assemble, top the crackers with one slice of Brie, a light layer of cranberry chutney, and four or five sugared cranberries. Garnish with fresh mint sprigs.

Makes about 16 bites

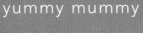

LIFE TIP

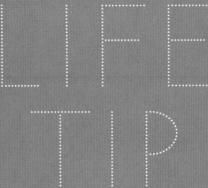

Don't wait for a holiday party to make a glamorous sparkling snack. Put on your sequins and call your fellow Yummy Mummy friends for an afternoon play date, or grab your sun hat and pack healthy treats for the beach or park. Adding a touch of sparkle, whether it's a quick coat of lip gloss or a stylish snack, can make moms feel yummy in the midst of piles of laundry and diapers.

I find that I'm a much happier mommy after our play dates with good friends and fun food. It's important for kids to have time to play with other children, but it's also important for moms to have support from other moms. I love adding a little extra sparkle to the everyday, and pretty appetizers are a great way to do just that.

The combination of goat cheese and blueberries is one of my favorites. The sweet berries are the perfect contrast to the tangy cheese. These crostini are a show-stopping spring and summer appetizer. Kids, like adults, are attracted to the beautiful glittery berries.

Sugared Blueberry Goat Cheese Crostini

1 cup water
1½ cups sugar
6 ounces fresh blueberries
1 loaf French bread, cut into ½-inch slices
5 ounces goat cheese, at room temperature
Small fresh basil leaves, for garnish

Stir ½ cup sugar into the water in a small saucepan over medium heat. Cook until the sugar dissolves completely, about 3 minutes. Pour into a medium bowl and let cool completely. Pour the blueberries into sugar syrup and gently toss to coat. Pour the remaining 1 cup sugar into a medium bowl or dish. Remove the blueberries with a slotted spoon and let the excess sugar syrup drip off. Place the blueberries in the sugar and gently toss to lightly coat. Remove and place on a tray to dry for 1 hour.

Place slices of bread on a baking sheet and lightly toast. Spread goat cheese on top of toasts. Top with sugared blueberries and garnish with basil.

Makes about 10 crostini

TIP

Exposing kids to entertaining is a good thing, as it's an opportunity to teach manners and important social skills. Teaching our kids etiquette and proper table manners is a gift they can use their whole life. Tai Tai had her three children set the table every night and politely greet guests at the door when they had company. Tai Tai, and later my mom, reminded her children even during casual weeknight family dinners at home of proper etiquette. I'm thankful to have acquired this knowledge as a child, as I have always felt comfortable eating at friends' houses, in upscale restaurants, and while traveling abroad, because I had been brought up knowing how to be polite in these situations.

I almost always have all the ingredients for this easy dip on hand. I keep the edamame in the freezer and garbanzo beans in the pantry. If guests show up unexpectedly or we are hungry for a last-minute snack, I can have a delicious healthy homemade dip ready in 10 minutes.

Effortless Edamame-Basil Hummus Dip

2 cups shelled cooked edamame
⅔ cup garbanzo beans (chickpeas), drained and rinsed
3 cloves garlic
½ cup fresh basil, plus more for garnish
¼ cup lemon juice
½ teaspoon salt
¼ teaspoon freshly cracked pepper
⅓ cup extra-virgin olive oil
Pita chips or carrots and celery for dipping

Reserve 1 tablespoon each of the edamame and garbanzo beans for garnish. In a food processor, blend the remaining edamame, the remaining garbanzo beans, the garlic, basil, lemon juice, salt, and pepper. Slowly pour the olive oil through the feed tube while the processor is on. Process until smooth and well blended. Add salt and pepper to taste.

Pour into a serving bowl and garnish with edamame, garbanzo beans, olive oil, and basil. Serve with pita chips and vegetables.

Makes about 3 cups

This hummus makes delicious "glue" to hold wraps together or spread for sandwiches. Try it on whole-grain toast with sliced tomatoes, avocado, and fresh spinach for a healthy sandwich.

You don't have to shell your own edamame. Many stores sell it already shelled in the freezer or refrigerated section.

Eggplant "Fries"

1 small globe eggplant
2 large egg whites
1 cup panko breadcrumbs
¼ cup grated Parmesan cheese
1 teaspoon chopped fresh parsley
½ teaspoon salt
¼ teaspoon freshly cracked pepper
1 tablespoon extra-virgin olive oil

Preheat the oven to 450°F. Line a cookie sheet with parchment paper.

Cut the eggplant in half crosswise. For each half, place the cut side down
and cut into ½-inch slices, then cut each slice lengthwise into ½-inch-wide
"fries." In a medium shallow bowl, whisk the egg whites until lightly beaten.
In another shallow medium bowl, stir together the breadcrumbs, Parmesan, parsley, salt, and pepper. Dip the eggplant pieces into the egg and let
the excess drip off. Place into the breadcrumb mixture and coat. Place on
the cookie sheet and drizzle with olive oil. Bake for 12 minutes, until golden
brown and crisp.

Serve immediately with marinara (Slow Cooker Veggie-Loaded Marinara,
page 137) or aioli sauce (store-bought works great) for dipping.

Serves 6

Baked Spinach and Artichoke Dip

10 ounces frozen chopped spinach, thawed and squeezed dry

8 ounces frozen artichoke hearts, thawed, drained, and sliced

½ cup light sour cream

1 large clove garlic, minced

½ cup fresh mozzarella cheese, patted dry and shredded or diced

½ cup grated Parmesan cheese

¼ teaspoon salt

¼ teaspoon freshly cracked pepper

1 baguette, cut into ½-inch slices

Preheat the oven to 375°F. Lightly coat an 8-inch baking dish with cooking spray.

In a medium bowl, stir together the spinach, artichokes, sour cream, garlic, ¼ cup mozzarella, ¼ cup Parmesan, salt, and pepper. Transfer the mixture to the baking dish, top with the remaining ¼ cup mozzarella and ¼ cup Parmesan, and bake for 30 to 35 minutes until bubbling and the cheese has started to brown.

Serve with sliced bread.

Serves 6

Roasting grapes is fun and unexpected, although very popular in the wine regions of Italy. I remember being surprised to find juicy grapes cooked into a dense olive oil cake in Tuscany years ago. Here the sweetness of the grapes balances the earthy truffle oil and rosemary, and the feta adds a salty kick. The flavors are just perfect, and this flatbread takes me right back to Tuscany every time.

Grape and Rosemary Flatbread

1 (16-ounce) homemade or store-bought pizza dough

1 tablespoon truffle oil

2 teaspoons fresh rosemary, chopped

⅔ cup red grapes, halved

½ teaspoon finishing salt

2 tablespoons crumbled feta cheese

I enjoy making homemade pizza dough, and the kids love kneading it for me. My favorite pizza dough recipe is by Wolfgang Puck. On especially busy nights, I will buy a prepared fresh pizza dough from the grocery store. Many pizzerias will also sell their dough—just ask!

Preheat the oven to 500°F. Line a baking sheet with parchment paper and lightly dust with flour.

Take the pizza dough out of refrigerator 30 minutes before using. With a sharp knife, cut the dough in half. Stretch the dough into two long rectangles (about 6 × 11 inches each) on the parchment paper. Brush with truffle oil. Sprinkle with rosemary, grapes, salt, and feta. Bake for 8 to 10 minutes. Remove from the oven and cut into slices.

Makes 2 flatbreads

Puff pastry is my secret weapon for effortless entertaining. A box can always be found in my freezer for last-minute play dates. I top it like a pizza, with cheese and any seasonal produce from thinly sliced zucchini, to caramelized onions, to sautéed mushrooms. In the winter I love to top the tarts with goat cheese and roasted beets. In the summer, my favorite toppings are sliced heirloom tomatoes of all colors.

Heirloom Tomato and Asiago Tartlets

1 sheet puff pastry, thawed according to box directions
¼ cup grated Asiago cheese
1 tablespoon fresh thyme leaves
3 medium heirloom tomatoes, thinly sliced
Salt and freshly cracked pepper to taste

Preheat the oven to 400°F. Line a cookie sheet with parchment paper.

Roll the puff pastry to about ⅛-inch thickness. Cut into 9 rectangles by slicing into thirds lengthwise and then again crosswise. Sprinkle each rectangle with cheese, leaving a ¼-inch border around the edges. Top the cheese with a small pinch of thyme leaves. Overlap 2 or 3 tomato slices over the cheese. Sprinkle with a pinch of salt and pepper. Bake for 15 to 20 minutes, until the pastry is puffed and golden. Garnish with additional thyme leaves.

Serves 6

Fruit and cheese are a delightful match. When peaches are sweet in the summer, I love to combine them with sharp Gorgonzola on salads, pizza, and here in elegant little purses. These purses are perfect bite-size bundles bursting with flavor. No one will ever guess just how easy they are to make.

Peach and Gorgonzola Phyllo Purses

1 (16-ounce) box phyllo dough, thawed
Cooking spray
5 ounces crumbled Gorgonzola cheese
2 large peaches
1 sprig rosemary
3 tablespoons honey

Preheat the oven to 350°F. Line a cookie sheet with parchment paper.

Lay the phyllo dough on the counter. Cover any dough not immediately being used with a damp paper towel, so that it doesn't dry out and become too brittle to work with. Lay 5 sheets of phyllo on top of each other, coating each layer lightly with cooking spray. With a sharp knife, cut the phyllo into 4-inch squares. Keep the exposed dough covered with another damp paper towel. Spoon 1 teaspoon of cheese onto the center of each rectangle.

Cut the peaches in half. Remove the pits and cut into ½-inch wedges and then crosswise into half-wedges. Top the cheese on each rectangle with a half-wedge of peach, 2 rosemary leaves, and a tiny dab of honey. Bring the phyllo up and around the peach and cheese filling, gently twisting and pressing together at the top. Repeat the process with remaining ingredients. Place the phyllo purses on the cookie sheet and bake until crisp and golden brown, about 13 minutes.

Makes about 20 purses

Fruit, cheese, and honey go so well together. This is my favorite winter combination of those simple ingredients. This snack is rather addictive and a favorite among my friends.

Pear, Humboldt Fog Cheese, and Honey Crisps

1 (6-ounce) package crisp crackers
4 ounces Humboldt Fog cheese
1 pear, cut into half-slices
2 tablespoons honey

With a cheese knife, spread a slice of cheese on each cracker. Top cheese with a single pear half-slice and drizzle with honey.

Serves 6 to 8

My favorite crackers for this recipe are Rosemary Raisin Pecan Raincoast Crisps by Lesley Stowe, available at Whole Foods and other grocery stores. Humboldt Fog cheese is also available at Whole Foods.

These cool shrimp boats are fresh and simple. They are perfect appetizers for any get-together, but I even like to pair them with a salad for dinner on warm summer nights when we're eating on the patio.

Quick Grilled Shrimp in Avocado Boats

1 clove garlic, minced

2 limes

1 tablespoon extra-virgin olive oil

¼ teaspoon salt

6 jumbo peeled, deveined shrimp

3 avocados, halved lengthwise and pits removed

½ cup cherry tomatoes, halved

¼ cup fresh cilantro, for garnish

Stir together the garlic, the juice of 1 lime, olive oil, and salt in a medium bowl. Add shrimp and toss to coat. Heat a grill pan over medium-high heat and lightly coat with cooking spray. Place the shrimp in the pan and cook until pink and opaque in the center, about 2 minutes per side.

Sprinkle the cut sides of the avocados with salt. If there is not enough room for the shrimp in the center of the avocados, scoop out a little of the flesh with a spoon. Place one shrimp inside each avocado hole. Fill the remaining space with tomatoes. Cut the remaining lime into thin wedges and place in avocados. Garnish with cilantro. Serve with forks.

Makes 6 boats

This elegant hors d'oeuvre takes 5 minutes to make and can be made up to 3 hours in advance and refrigerated. Sweet raspberries and pecans balance the tangy goat cheese and crunchy endive. I served these fancy finger foods last year for an afternoon of baking ginger-bread men with friends. They were a hit with both the moms and kids, and not a single one was left over.

Raspberry Endives with Candied Pecans

2 endives
4 ounces goat cheese, at room temperature
6 ounces fresh raspberries
¼ cup candied pecans, roughly chopped

Trim 1 inch off the bottoms of the endives. Separate, rinse, and dry the leaves. Spread about 1 teaspoon of goat cheese on the lower half of the endive leaves. Place 2 raspberries on top of the cheese. Sprinkle with pecans.

Makes about 15 appetizers

Strawberries and balsamic vinegar are a popular Italian combination. My family loves eating balsamic strawberries over vanilla ice cream, but I wanted to make a daytime snack that was similar to one of my other favorite appetizers—tomato bruschetta. This version was a success with my husband and kids and a refreshing summertime treat.

Balsamic Strawberry Bruschetta

1½ cups chopped strawberries
3 teaspoons balsamic vinegar
¼ cup fresh basil, sliced
1 loaf of French bread, sliced and lightly toasted

Place the chopped strawberries, balsamic vinegar, and basil in a small serving bowl. Toss together. Top the bread slices with the strawberry mixture.

Makes about 15 bruschette

soups

A BOWL OF COMFORT

When I think of comforting foods, soup is the first thing that comes to mind. The quintessential food for colds, soup is loved for its warmth, vitamins, and ease on an upset tummy or sore throat. As a child I remember asking for chicken soup, salty white crackers, and ginger ale anytime I felt a cold coming on. At times, craving that solace, I even pretended to be sick just so I had an excuse to ask for soup. Bringing the soup close to my face and feeling the bowl warming my hands and the brothy steam enveloping my face instantly made me feel better even before I had a taste.

Most of the time when I ask my husband, Phil, what he wants for dinner, he responds, "Soup and grilled cheese?" At the beginning of our marriage I took this to mean he didn't want me to go to any trouble. Or perhaps he was avoiding the massive amount of dishes and splatters I leave in the wake of my cooking adventures. Now I realize he really just wants soup. There really is nothing better than "soup and grilled cheese" to wash away the stress of a long day. My girls often ask for soup for dinner too, and although they probably don't realize it yet, they feel that same comfort in soup that I remember as a child.

As a mom with young children, I seem to constantly have friends who are having babies. Onesies and toys are always appreciated postnatal gifts, but nothing is more comforting, helpful, or thoughtful than a home-cooked meal. Dropping off dinner for a new mom means she can spend those precious first few days and weeks bonding with her new baby, catching up on sleep, and recovering from the marathon that is childbirth. It means nourishment and normalcy for baby's older siblings and mom and dad. It means mom doesn't have to take a newborn out to a grocery store, where well-intentioned but inappropriate strangers can't help but touch the baby. Casseroles are the traditional go-to dish to bring to friends, but soup is my dish of choice for new moms or friends in need.

I have a friend, Holley, who is known as "the Southern belle in Santa Barbara." She once told a story about how, in the South, if someone was going through a difficult time, there would be a line at the front door of people bringing food. After the births of my girls, I was lucky to have friends like her set up a food tree. For three weeks I had a meal delivered every other day. I get the feeling that my friends are exceptional, and that outside of the way Holley describes Southern hospitality most people don't go out of their way to bring dinner to friends often enough. I try to remember how helpful a delivered dinner can be. Food nourishes our bodies and our souls, making it the best gift we can give. Soup, with its inherent cozy feel, may be the perfect drop-off dinner. When you give a pot of soup, you're not just giving food. You're giving a feeling that can't be bought. One of the most beautiful qualities of food is the way it connects people. Soup is an easy way to bond over good food and show someone that you care.

A big pot of soup simmering on the stove makes our house feel like a home. The air is infused the smell of herbs and spices. The gentle bubbling sound is a relaxing prelude to dinnertime. Every time I lift the lid to stir or add another herb, the soup has changed slightly. Like a piece of art or a story, it's constantly evolving.

On days when we are away from the house, I throw all the ingredients for soup in the slow cooker. When I get home, I can't help but smile at the warm smells filling our home. Dinner is ready without any work. I love that I can make a huge batch of healthy soup for dinner and the girls can take leftovers in a thermos to school. If there is still soup left over, I freeze it for another day.

Try inventing your own soups using leftover vegetables at the end of the week. Simply sauté onions with any vegetables, add fresh or dried herbs, and chicken or vegetable stock. Stir in shredded cooked chicken, quinoa, beans, pasta, or rice for a complete one-dish meal. The flavors and colors of premade soups found in the grocery store don't come anywhere close to those of homemade soups. Once you realize how easy and delicious homemade soup is, you'll be hooked just as I am.

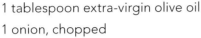

Lentil Soup

1 tablespoon extra-virgin olive oil
1 onion, chopped
2 carrots, chopped
2 celery stalks, chopped
1 large russet potato, diced
2 cloves garlic, minced
2 teaspoons herbs of Provence
8 cups vegetable stock
2 cups dried lentils
1 (14.5-ounce) can diced tomatoes
1 cup fresh spinach
Salt and freshly cracked pepper to taste
¼ cup grated Parmesan cheese

Lentils are low-calorie legumes high in protein, fiber, vitamins, and minerals. They keep you feeling full and are good for your health.

Heat the olive oil in a large pot over medium heat. Add the onion, carrots, celery, potato, and a pinch of salt and pepper. Sauté the vegetables until softened, about 5 minutes. Add the garlic and herbs and sauté 1 minute longer. Add the stock, lentils, and tomatoes. Simmer over low heat, covered, until the lentils are cooked, about 45 minutes. Stir in the spinach. Season to taste with salt and pepper. Serve with Parmesan cheese.

Serves 4 to 6

The bright color and flavor of fresh pea soup are a wonderfully refreshing change from heartier soups. This dish can be on the table in 15 minutes and is the perfect accompaniment for fish or chicken in the spring and summer. My kids and I prefer this simpler version, but if you would like to try traditional Minted English Pea Soup, simply add ¼ cup fresh mint before blending.

Easy Peasy Fresh Pea Soup

1 tablespoon extra-virgin olive oil
½ shallot, chopped
1 clove garlic, minced
3 cups fresh shucked peas (about 2 pounds of whole peas)
1 teaspoon salt
2 cups chicken or vegetable broth
¼ cup crème fraiche, for garnish (optional)
Pea shoots, for garnish (optional)

Heat the olive oil in a large pot over medium heat. Add the chopped shallot and sauté until softened, about 5 minutes. Add the garlic and sauté 1 minute. Add the peas, salt, and broth. Cover and simmer until the peas have softened, about 10 minutes. Let cool for 5 minutes. Remove 2 tablespoons of the peas and reserve for garnish. Carefully transfer the pea mixture to a blender and puree.

Serve warm or chilled. Garnish with a drizzle of extra-virgin olive oil, a dollop of crème fraiche, and a few whole peas and pea shoots, if desired.

Serves 4

Some grocery stores now carry fresh English peas refrigerated in the produce section. Alternately, good-quality frozen peas could be substituted in a pinch.

My mom makes the most delicious salmon chowder. It always reminds me how tasty leeks are. The combination of tomatoes and cream creates a pretty pink base.

Salmon Chowder

2 tablespoons extra-virgin olive oil

1 cup diced russet potatoes (although any type on hand will do)

1 cup sliced leeks

1 cup sliced button or cremini mushrooms

2 cloves garlic, minced

1 cup dry white wine

1 (14.5-ounce) can crushed tomatoes

3 cups fish or vegetable stock

1 cup half and half, plus 1 tablespoon for garnish

1 cup fat-free plain Greek yogurt

¼ cup fresh parsley, chopped

1 tablespoon fresh dill, chopped

Salt and freshly cracked pepper to taste

1 pound wild salmon, cut into about 2-inch pieces

Heat the olive oil in a large pot over medium heat. Add the potatoes, leeks, and mushrooms. Sauté the vegetables until softened, about 5 minutes. Add the garlic and continue to stir for 1 minute. Add the white wine and simmer until most of the liquid has cooked off. Stir in the tomatoes, fish or vegetable stock, half and half, yogurt, parsley, and dill and bring to a low simmer. Season to taste with salt and pepper. Add the salmon and simmer until just cooked through, about 5 minutes.

Ladle into bowls and garnish with drops of half and half and parsley or dill, if desired.

Serves 6

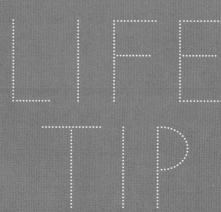

yummy mummy

LIFE TIP

Thinking about this creamy soup makes me feel calm and relaxed and transports me to my parents' kitchen table. A bowl of soup at home feels warm and casual and makes everyone feel comfortable. Knowing that the soup was made with caring hands makes it taste even better. I like to make this soup pretty and fun for my husband and kids by dragging a knife through drops of cream to make hearts on top. It's the small touches that can often make a big difference. I hope my girls will have memories of comforting soup dinners around our kitchen table the way I have of my mom's Salmon Chowder.

Making soup for family or friends is an easy way to tell them you love them, you're sorry, get well, thank you, or that you're thinking of them. If I'm planning on taking soup to a friend, I make a big pot of soup early in the day, let it cool, and pour half into a glass storage container. I place the soup in a large gift basket with a loaf of fresh store-bought bread, a salad mix, a few cookies, a bottle of wine, and a note. It's a small effort, but anyone would be touched by this thoughtful home-made gift.

I fell in love with Pappa al Pomodoro, or Bread and Tomato Soup, at a restaurant in Florence, Italy, called Ristoro di Cambi. I started making a similar soup at home in the summer when the tomatoes are at their sweetest. I now leave out the bread and add white beans and kale to boost the nutritional content. Make this soup a complete meal with a hunk of crusty bread.

Tuscan Roasted Tomato, White Bean, and Kale Soup

2½ pounds ripe Roma or local red tomatoes (about 10 medium), halved

1 red bell pepper, halved, core and seeds removed

1 shallot, peeled and quartered

4 large cloves garlic, peeled

2 tablespoons extra-virgin olive oil, plus more for drizzling over soup

Salt and freshly cracked pepper to taste

3 cups vegetable broth

1 cup packed fresh basil leaves, plus more for garnish

2 cups baby kale

1 (15-ounce) can cannellini beans, drained and rinsed

1 tablespoon balsamic vinegar

1 cup croutons (optional)

Baby kale is milder than traditional kale and is available at many farmers' markets and gourmet grocery stores, such as Whole Foods. If baby kale is unavailable, use Tuscan kale, torn into bite-size pieces.

Preheat the oven to 450°F. Place the tomatoes, pepper, shallot, and garlic on a large rimmed baking pan. Drizzle with olive oil and toss to coat. Sprinkle with salt and pepper. Roast for 25 minutes, or until very soft and browned in areas.

Transfer the vegetables to a large pot over low heat. Add the broth and basil. With an immersion blender, puree the tomato mixture directly in the pot. Alternately, puree the vegetables in a standard blender or food processor and then pour them back into the pot. Bring to a simmer, stir in the kale, beans, and balsamic vinegar and cook just until the kale has wilted. Season to taste with salt and pepper.

Ladle into bowls, drizzle with olive oil, and garnish with more basil and croutons.

Serves 6

The toppings make this soup fun for both kids and adults to eat. Crunchy tortilla strips, avocados, and cheese offer something for everyone. Even kids who typically resist vegetables are sure to gobble this veggie-rich soup right up.

Veggie Tortilla Soup with Quinoa

2 tablespoons extra-virgin olive oil

1 onion, chopped

2 cloves garlic, minced

3 carrots, chopped

2 celery stalks, chopped

Salt and freshly cracked pepper to taste

1 teaspoon ground cumin

1 teaspoon ground coriander

28 ounces canned crushed tomatoes

4 cups vegetable stock

1 zucchini, chopped

⅓ cup uncooked quinoa

3 corn tortillas

1 tablespoon extra-virgin olive oil

1 to 2 avocados, peeled, pitted, and diced

½ cup fresh cilantro, chopped

½ cup grated cheddar cheese

½ cup sour cream

1 lime, cut into wedges

Protein boost! Quinoa is a great source of vegetarian protein, but feel free to replace the quinoa with shredded cooked chicken breast when the soup is almost done.

For the soup, heat the olive oil in a large pot over medium heat. Add the onion, garlic, carrots, and celery. Season with salt and pepper. Cook, stirring occasionally, until carrots are tender, about 7 minutes. Stir in the cumin and coriander. Add the tomatoes, vegetable stock, and zucchini. Bring to a low simmer and stir in the quinoa. Simmer uncovered until the quinoa is cooked, 10 to 15 minutes, stirring occasionally. Season to taste with salt and pepper.

For the tortilla strips, preheat the oven to 425°F. Cut the tortillas into ⅛-inch strips, drizzle with 1 tablespoon of olive oil, and sprinkle with salt. Toast on a cookie sheet, turning once, until golden, about 5 minutes.

Place the tortilla strips, avocados, cilantro, cheese, sour cream, and lime wedges in individual bowls and offer as toppings.

Serves 6

Chili is always a crowd-pleaser, but it doesn't have to be fatty and include meat to be delicious. Add any vegetables you have on hand. We love the hearty sweetness sweet potato contributes in the fall and winter months. This chili is not too spicy, but when cooking for younger children, start with slightly less than the called-for amount of chili powder and add the rest, if desired, after tasting.

Veggie-Loaded Chili

Time-saving tip: Place all the ingredients except for the garnishes in a slow cooker in the morning and cook for 6 hours on low.

2 tablespoons extra-virgin olive oil

1 onion, chopped

2 cloves garlic, minced

2 carrots, chopped

2 celery stalks, chopped

1 sweet potato, peeled and diced

Salt and freshly cracked pepper to taste

1 tablespoon chili powder

1 teaspoon cumin

1 red bell pepper, diced

2 tablespoons tomato paste

28 ounces canned diced tomatoes in juice

3 cups vegetable broth

1 (15-ounce) can kidney beans, drained and rinsed

1 (15-ounce) can black beans, drained and rinsed

Fresh cilantro, for garnish

Green onions, sliced, for garnish

Sour cream, for garnish

Heat the olive oil in a large pot over medium heat. Add the onion, garlic, carrots, celery, and sweet potato. Season lightly with salt and pepper and cook, stirring, until the vegetables soften, about 7 minutes. Stir in the chili powder, cumin, and bell pepper. Add the tomato paste, tomatoes, broth, and beans. Bring to a simmer and cook uncovered over low heat until thickened, about 30 minutes. Garnish with cilantro, green onions, and sour cream.

Serves 6

salads and vegetables

SALAD GIRLS

My girls and I call ourselves "salad girls." For some, salad is the boring, unappetizing meal that is reluctantly gulped down for health's sake. For others, like my girls and me, it's the refreshing, sweet, savory, crunchy lunch or dinner we love. Salad is a canvas for all sorts of creative toppings and dressings. When we're out and about, the most requested pick-up lunch from my kids is a salad-bar creation from Whole Foods. The kids get to choose their favorite ingredients, and everyone is happy. Though many parents would not think to give their kids salad for lunch, it may just be the perfect kid-friendly meal.

I believe that those who think they dislike vegetables just haven't been eating the right vegetables at the right times or haven't learned what to do with them. I learned to really love salad while living in Italy, where I made a salad filled with just-picked produce, balsamic vinaigrette, and pecorino cheese for lunch every day. It was there that I learned the importance of local and seasonal cooking. On my daily walk back to my apartment, I would stop at a local produce stand and pick up a bag of whatever vegetables had just been picked. Next I stopped at the *forno*, or bakery, where I bought a loaf of crusty Tuscan bread that had just come out of the wood-fired oven to use to soak up any leftover balsamic vinegar and olive oil that remained on my salad plate. Once in a bout of homesickness, I made the mistake of seeking out a California avocado. It was outrageously expensive and, sadly, tasteless. I had learned my lesson—seasonal and local is always best.

Years later, my husband, Phil, and I traveled back to the Emilia-Romagna and Tuscany regions of Italy. We sped around on a Ducati motorcycle (me on the back) and then spent a few days in Bologna for a conference. Phil was in meetings all day, so I decided to explore all the best food shops and farmers' markets in Bologna. It was at a fruit stand there that I picked up a fragrant cantaloupe. It was still warm from the vine and heavy with juice. It was so different from the cold, hard, flavorless supermarket melons I was accustomed to. I also stopped at a famous deli I found in my pocket guide and proudly asked for a quarter pound of prosciutto di Parma and pasta salad in my broken Italian. The sweet man behind the counter said, "Brava," as he handed me my parchment-wrapped packages. Back at the hotel, I set out a small picnic of cantaloupe, prosciutto, and pasta salad. I didn't need a recipe, and I didn't need to cook anything. The produce was so good that it didn't need any help. To this day I think that was the best meal I have ever had, and it all started with a freshly picked cantaloupe.

In Santa Barbara we are lucky to have an abundance of beautiful fresh produce year-round. Wherever you are, there should be delicious food at your farmers' markets and local grocers if you buy what is in season. Strolling the farmers' markets can be incredibly uplifting, like a mini vacation. Take in the colors and textures, the people and sounds. Meet the farmers and ask about what they are selling. Often they have fascinating stories about how they procured the seeds for a particular crop. When my kids were babies and getting to the farmers' market was too hard, I had a weekly produce box delivered from a local CSA (Community Supported Agriculture). If you use these ingredients for salads throughout the week, the way your salad will evolve throughout the seasons is really beautiful. Kids quickly become curious and eager to find out what is in the CSA box, growing in the garden, or popping up at the farmers' market.

Kids are often the most unwavering veggie haters. My theory is that they've heard from too many adults that "kids hate vegetables," rather than that they have an innate distain for them. Like all aspects of education, kids' attitudes about foods are often our self-fulfilling prophecies. We tell kids they don't like broccoli, onions, and garlic—so they don't. What happens if we tell them that these foods are beautiful and delicious from the start? If we grow these vegetables with them, and we let them choose them at the farmers' market? In my experience, kids who are educated about and exposed to good-quality, seasonal, local fruits and vegetables actually love them. My four-year-old, for example, will not come near cheese, but routinely asks for salads for lunch, Brussels sprouts for dinner, and extra onions on everything. Kids don't need their food to be dumbed down. Just like adults, they actually like flavorful foods.

I try to eat salad for lunch every day. There are times when I am so busy or distracted that I end up eating what I also love—some form of bread and cheese. But I am always struck by how much better I feel when I have salad for lunch. I have more energy to run around with my little ones, and I don't feel weighed down. With a little planning, salad can be a creative and exciting meal packed not only with vegetables, but protein, fruits, nuts, cheeses, and grains too. The key to good salads is mixing up the flavors and textures. In the summer, my salads are filled with berries, stone fruits, and tomatoes. In the winter I use dried cranberries, blue cheese, and pumpkin seeds. Salad is so much more than just lettuce. Try creating salads topped with your kids' favorite foods. They may surprise you and start asking for salad for lunch instead of a burger or grilled cheese.

The key to eating a lot of healthy foods is to have them readily available and easy to prepare. When we come home hungry and do not have healthy foods immediately available, it's easy to head straight for the cookie jar. The idea behind the Refrigerator Salad Bar is that there is always an opportunity to throw together a customized salad in less than 5 minutes. Prepare favorite seasonal produce, nuts, dried fruit, and protein on Sunday night. Keep these ingredients on a tray in covered bowls in the refrigerator to use throughout the week on top of baby spinach or mixed green lettuce.

The Refrigerator Salad Bar

Start with a base of greens. Choose one or two additions from each of the categories to quickly build a healthy complete meal that's rich in flavor and texture. These are some of my favorite salad toppings—use them for inspiration and ideas for your own Refrigerator Salad Bar.

Vegetables

Tomato, chopped, or cherry
    tomatoes
Peas
Cucumber, sliced
Broccoli, steamed or raw
Beets
Carrots, grated or chopped
Leftover grilled or roasted vege-
    tables (e.g., zucchini, egg
    plant, sweet potato)

Fruit

Avocado
Strawberries, sliced
Blueberries
Raspberries
Apples, chopped
Pears, sliced
Pomegranate seeds
Dried cranberries
Grapes
Peaches, chopped

Protein

Hard-boiled eggs

Cooked quinoa

Cooked beans (garbanzo, kidney, black)

Steamed edamame

Tofu, cubed

Cooked lentils

Cheese (grated cheddar or other hard
   cheese, crumbled blue, goat, or other
   soft cheese)

Tuna

Seeds and Nuts

Walnuts

Pecans

Pepitas (pumpkin seeds)

Pine nuts

Pistachios

Sesame seeds

Chia seeds

Flaxseeds

Toddlers love to make their own decisions. Defiant tantrums can often be avoided by giving options rather than making demands. Similarly, we can help toddlers make their own healthy choices by giving them wholesome food options. My favorite way to implement this is by filling a sectioned storage container with finger foods. I use a baby-food storage container. Fill the sections with fruits, vegetables, and protein. Bring out the toddler salad bar at snack time or lunchtime. It should last for several days. Serve only age-appropriate foods, and ask your pediatrician before starting any new foods you are unsure about.

The Refrigerator Salad Bar for Toddlers

Favorite Toddler Salad Bar Ingredients

Hard-boiled egg, diced

Edamame, steamed

Lentils, steamed

Tofu, diced

Cheddar cheese, diced

Peas, steamed

Broccoli, steamed and cut into
small florets

Sweet potato, roasted and cubed

Carrots, steamed or roasted and
cubed

Grapes, halved

Raisins

Blueberries, halved for babies

Strawberries, diced

Avocado, diced

Crackers

Cheerios

Edible apple bowls make this the cutest salad I've ever had. These
salads are perfect for a fun afternoon snack with kids or an elegant
appetizer to wow dinner-party guests.

Apple, Pomegranate, and Avocado Salad in Apple Bowls

4 large apples

1 lemon

1 cup pomegranate seeds

2 avocados, peeled, pitted, and diced

3 tablespoons crumbled blue cheese

1 tablespoon apple cider vinegar

Slice the tops off the apples with a knife. Using a melon
baller or spoon, carefully scoop out the apple flesh, leaving about ¼-inch-thick apple shell. Squeeze lemon juice
over the cut surfaces of the apples to prevent browning.
Chop the apple flesh. In a medium bowl, gently toss
together the apple flesh, pomegranate seeds, avocado,
blue cheese, and apple cider vinegar. Carefully spoon
the mixture back into the hollowed-out apples.

Makes 4 salad bowls

yummy mummy

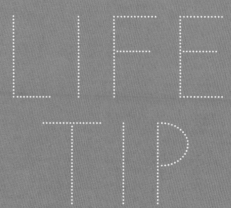

LIFE TIP

Every year my group of mommy friends and I go out to dinner with our husbands for our "holiday work party." We decided that even though we don't work in offices, our 24/7 jobs as mothers should be celebrated. We shop for sexy new dresses and put on our highest pair of heels. For one night we ditch the diaper bags for clutch purses that could never hold the sippy cups and baby paraphernalia we usually carry around. We laugh, take silly pictures, eat dinner without anyone sitting in our laps, and dance the night away. As moms, we have the best and hardest job in the world and deserve a "work party" too.

Try getting together for an adults-only evening out with friends every once in a while. Whether it's a dinner party after the kids have gone to bed or dinner at a favorite restaurant, getting dressed up and socializing with friends is good for moms. It's also a great opportunity for dads, who may not get together with other parents as often as moms do, to bond with each other.

This salad is a favorite with my kids. The sweet grapes and creamy fat-free dressing attract even those who think they don't like broccoli. And it's easy to pack any extra in lunchboxes since, unlike other salads, it doesn't get too soggy. The large number of antioxidants in this salad is just what preschool and school-age children need to keep their immune systems strong.

Broccoli Antioxidant Salad

¼ cup nonfat plain Greek yogurt

1 tablespoon Dijon mustard

1 teaspoon lemon juice

1 teaspoon honey

2 cups broccoli florets

1 cup grapes

1 carrot, sliced

1 celery stalk, sliced

1 avocado, peeled, pitted, and sliced

1 green onion, sliced

¼ cup toasted walnut pieces

Salt and freshly cracked pepper to taste

For the dressing, in a small bowl stir together the yogurt, mustard, lemon juice, and honey. Set aside.

Bring ¾ of an inch of water to a simmer in a large saucepan with a steamer basket. Add the broccoli, cover, and cook until tender-crisp, about 2 minutes. Immediately transfer the broccoli to ice water to stop the cooking. Drain and pat the cooled broccoli dry with a paper towel.

Place the broccoli in a medium bowl. Add the grapes, carrot, celery, avocado, green onion, and walnuts. Pour the dressing over broccoli mixture and toss to coat. Season to taste with salt and pepper.

Serves 4

original yummy mummy

TIP

To raise physically and emotionally healthy kids, require them to play sports. My grandmother competed in field hockey and swim meets and believes sports are key in building character.

My parents followed suit and made sports compulsory in my life, and I'm so glad they did. Sports are very important not only to ingrain a healthy active lifestyle, but to teach life lessons about how to interact with others, work as a team, and even deal with losing. Participating in after-school sports means that kids are busy with healthy activities instead of getting into trouble.

Some friends seem surprised to hear that my kids often ask for Brussels sprouts with dinner. Boiled Brussels sprouts can be mushy and tasteless. Brussels sprouts roasted with olive oil and salt and pepper, however, become crispy on the outside, tender on the inside, and loved by kids and adults. I like to combine Brussels sprouts with butternut squash, as the squash adds a buttery sweetness. Make this scrumptious side dish in the fall and winter when Brussels sprouts and butternut squash are in season. Kids particularly like looking at and pulling the sprouts off the stalk. My girls like to pretend the Brussels sprout stalk is a fairy ladder.

Roasted Brussels Sprouts and Butternut Squash with Cranberries and Pine Nuts

1 small butternut squash

2 cups Brussels sprouts, halved lengthwise

2 tablespoons extra-virgin olive oil

½ teaspoon salt

¼ teaspoon freshly cracked pepper

¼ cup dried cranberries

¼ cup pine nuts, toasted

Preheat the oven to 400°F.

Using a vegetable peeler, peel the butternut squash. Cut the squash in half lengthwise and use a spoon to remove the seeds. Cut the squash into 2-inch cubes. On a large rimmed baking pan, toss the Brussels sprouts with the butternut squash and olive oil. Sprinkle with salt and pepper. Roast for 20 to 25 minutes until the vegetables are tender and lightly browned.

Transfer the vegetables to a large bowl and gently toss in the cranberries and sprinkle with pine nuts. Serve immediately.

Serves 4

Brussels sprouts are part of the important cruciferous vegetable family. Cruciferous vegetables are high in vitamins and minerals and may reduce the risk of cancer. Other cruciferous vegetables include broccoli, cauliflower, cabbage, and kale. Try to eat several servings of cruciferous vegetables every week.

This salad is one of my favorite lunchtime meals. The sweet and salty pecans add a wonderful crunch to the creamy burrata, fresh greens, and tomatoes.

Burrata, Tomato, Candied Pecan, and Mixed Greens Salad

½ cup extra-virgin olive oil
¼ cup balsamic vinegar
5 ounces mixed green baby lettuces
1 pound small tomatoes, halved (baby heirloom tomatoes or cherry tomatoes preferred)
½ cup candied pecans
2 (4-ounce) balls burrata cheese
Freshly cracked pepper to taste

In a small bowl, whisk together the oil and vinegar for the vinaigrette. Place the greens, tomatoes, and pecans in a large bowl. Toss with about ¼ cup of the dressing. Cover any leftover dressing with plastic wrap and save for another day. Divide the salad among the plates. Cut the burrata balls in half and place a half on each salad. Sprinkle with pepper, if desired.

Serves 4

Burrata is fresh mozzarella cheese with cream in the middle, making it softer than other mozzarella cheese. Burrata is available at Trader Joe's, Whole Foods, and other grocery stores.

Cobb salad is an American favorite, but it can be high in fat, calories, and nitrites when it is covered with bacon and turkey. My version is healthy but filling, and you won't miss the meat. Our family loves this salad for a light dinner. I love it because it's an easy one-bowl meal.

Veggie Cobb Salad

I served this salad for lunch to a group of moms with babies, and it was a very well received, easy make-ahead meal. I presented my Veggie Cobb Salad on a large platter and served it with a glass of champagne, plus bakery-bought cookies for dessert. Elegant entertaining can be as simple as a salad.

¼ cup extra-virgin olive oil

2 tablespoons Dijon mustard

1 tablespoon honey

1 clove garlic, minced

Juice of ½ lemon

8 ounces romaine lettuce, chopped

4 hard-boiled eggs, quartered

1 cup cherry tomatoes, halved

½ cup crumbled blue cheese

2 avocados, peeled, pitted, and cut into bite-size pieces

1 cup croutons

For the dressing, place the olive oil, mustard, honey, garlic, and lemon juice in a small bowl and whisk to combine. Place the lettuce in a large bowl. Place the eggs, tomatoes, blue cheese, avocados, and croutons in rows on top of the lettuce. Serve with the dressing.

Serves 4 to 6

Roasted Green Beans and Cherry Tomatoes

1 pound green beans, ends trimmed

1 pound (about 2 cups) cherry tomatoes

4 cloves garlic, peeled and halved

2 tablespoons extra-virgin olive oil

½ teaspoon coarse sea salt

¼ teaspoon freshly cracked pepper

Preheat the oven to 400°F. Place the green beans, tomatoes, and garlic on a large rimmed baking pan. Drizzle with olive oil and sprinkle with salt and pepper. Toss to coat. Roast for 12 to 15 minutes, until green beans are tender-crisp. Serve immediately.

Serves 4

Take care not to overcook green beans or they lose their bright green color and become mushy. Properly cooked fresh green beans are nothing like the canned variety, so if you think you don't like them, give them another try.

Beets become as sweet as candy after roasting. I choose a variety of colors of beets for a beautiful salad. After roasting and slipping the skins off, I am always amazed by the intensity of the bright pink, purple, and yellow colors. I roast a big batch of beets on Sunday after the farmers' market and we use them in salads and lunchboxes all week. Roasted beets are a favorite with my kids on their own or in a salad like this one.

Colorful Kale and Roasted Beet Salad

⅓ cup extra-virgin olive oil, plus 1 tablespoon
2 tablespoons champagne vinegar
Juice of 1 tangerine
Salt and freshly cracked pepper to taste
8 beets, various colors
3 ounces mixed baby greens
2 ounces lacinato kale (Tuscan kale), thinly sliced
1 to 2 tangerines, peeled and sectioned
2 ounces goat cheese, crumbled
¼ cup slivered almonds

To make the dressing, whisk ⅓ cup olive oil, champagne vinegar, and tangerine juice together in a small bowl. Season to taste with salt and pepper.

To roast the beets, preheat the oven to 400°F. Cut the greens off the beets and discard. Drizzle the beets with 1 tablespoon olive oil and wrap in foil or place in a Dutch oven and cover. Roast in the oven until fork tender, 40 minutes to 1 hour or more, depending on the size of the beets. Cool and peel the beets. Cut into quarters.

Place the greens and kale in a large bowl. Add the tangerine pieces, goat cheese, and almonds. Drizzle the vinaigrette over the salad and toss. Top the salad with the roasted beets.

Serves 4 to 6

Fresh cherries add a unique sweet juicy bite and beautiful color that are the perfect complement to nutty quinoa. This salad is one of my favorites for summertime lunches.

Quinoa Salad with Cherries

¼ cup extra-virgin olive oil

2 tablespoons balsamic vinegar

5 ounces fresh baby spinach

2 cups cooked quinoa

1½ cups fresh cherries, halved and pitted

½ cup crumbled feta cheese

¼ cup pumpkin seeds (or pistachios, sliced almonds, pine nuts, or other favorite nuts)

In a large bowl whisk together the olive oil, balsamic vinegar, and a pinch of salt and pepper. Toss the spinach with the vinaigrette. Top with the quinoa, cherries, feta, and pumpkin seeds.

Serves 4 to 6

The first week in August the city of Santa Barbara celebrates its Spanish history with "Old Spanish Days Fiesta." During this time, the whole city is abuzz with parties, flamenco dancing performances, kids cracking confetti eggs on each other's heads, and grilled corn and churros. I came up with this salad one year around Fiesta time, and it became an instant favorite with my family. This is an easy and healthy dinner perfect for outdoor cooking and dining.

Grilled Shrimp and Corn Salad

1 pound large peeled, deveined shrimp

1 ounce tequila

Juice of 2 limes

3 ears of corn, husks removed

2 heads romaine lettuce, chopped

½ cup black beans, drained and rinsed

½ cup cherry tomatoes, halved

1 avocado, sliced

¼ cup favorite salad dressing

Chopped fresh cilantro, for garnish

Sliced lime, for garnish

Tortilla chips (optional)

Cherry tomatoes are one of the easiest plants to grow. Put a couple of cherry tomato plants in the ground or in pots in the spring and watch your kids delightfully pluck juicy tomatoes all summer long.

Thread the shrimp on skewers and place in a baking dish. Coat with tequila and lime juice and marinate 15 minutes. Oil and preheat a grill or grill pan to medium-high heat. Brush the corn with olive oil and sprinkle with salt and pepper. Place the shrimp and corn on the grill and grill about 3 minutes per side until cooked through. Cool slightly. Remove the shrimp from skewers and slice the kernels off the cobs.

In a large bowl, toss the lettuce with the beans, tomatoes, avocado, and dressing. Arrange grilled shrimp and corn on top and garnish with cilantro and lime. Serve with tortilla chips, if desired.

Serves 4

This fresh starter is a beautiful way to use summer's best produce. Salty feta cheese complements the sweet tomatoes, basil, and creamy avocado perfectly.

Tomato, Basil, Avocado, and Feta Stacks

2 avocados
Salt and freshly cracked pepper to taste
2 red heirloom tomatoes, thinly sliced
2 yellow heirloom tomatoes, thinly sliced
2 tablespoons extra-virgin olive oil
2 teaspoons balsamic vinegar
4 ounces feta cheese
1 cup fresh basil leaves

With a small knife, cut the avocados in half crosswise. Remove the pits. Using a spoon, carefully scoop out the avocado flesh in one piece from each half. Cut into thin slices crosswise. Lightly sprinkle tomatoes and avocado with salt and pepper and drizzle with olive oil and balsamic vinegar. Cut the feta into thin slices. Layer the tomatoes, avocado, feta, and basil in stacks on plates.

Makes 4 stacks

If you love Caprese salad, feel free to trade the feta in this recipe for fresh mozzarella slices and omit the avocado.

I don't think any kid could resist these Italian-style zucchini boats
filled with cheese. They make a great vegetable side dish when
zucchini is abundant in the summer.

Cheesy Stuffed Zucchini

3 zucchini

1 cup ricotta cheese

½ cup grated Parmesan cheese

2 tablespoons minced fresh basil

¼ teaspoon salt

⅛ teaspoon freshly cracked pepper

Preheat the oven to 425°F.

Cut the zucchini in half lengthwise. Using a small spoon, scoop out the
seeds to make a well. In a small bowl, stir together the ricotta, ¼ cup
Parmesan, basil, salt, and pepper. With a spoon, smooth ricotta mixture
into the zucchini wells. Sprinkle the ricotta mixture with the remaining ¼ cup
Parmesan.

Place the zucchini, cheese side up, on a rimmed baking pan and bake for
13 minutes, until cheese has browned.

Serves 6

Zucchini is my
favorite crop to
grow, because it is
almost fail-proof
even for those of
us who are not
blessed with a
green thumb.
One zucchini
plant produces
plenty of zuc-
chini, and I love
using its bright
yellow flowers
on top of salads,
pastas, pizzas,
and stuffed with
cheese.

Lemon zest and juice brighten the flavors of asparagus, one of my favorite springtime ingredients. I love to serve quick Lemony Asparagus as a side dish with fish or chicken.

Lemony Asparagus

1 tablespoon extra-virgin olive oil
1 bunch asparagus
Salt and freshly cracked pepper to taste
Zest of 1 lemon
Juice of ½ lemon

Heat the oil in a frying pan over medium-high heat. Add the asparagus to the pan. Season with salt and pepper and cook, turning occasionally, until tender-crisp, about 5 minutes. Add the lemon zest and juice and toss to coat. Adjust salt and pepper to taste. Serve immediately.

Serves 4

meatless main dishes

Mom's Best Quiche

Black Bean Burgers with Mango-Avocado Salsa

Cauliflower Mac and Cheese

Fiesta Burritos

Favorite Guacamole

Spaghetti with Roasted Butternut Squash, Peas, and Sage Pesto

Sage Pesto

Dad's Garlic Ricotta Calzone

Summer Squash Rainbow Pizza

Honey-Curry Glazed Vegetables and Garbanzos

Grilled Eggplant Stuffed with Spinach and Cheese

Farmers' Market Pasta

Southwestern Quinoa Stuffed Peppers

Baked Spaghetti Squash and "Meatballs"

Slow Cooker Veggie-Loaded Marinara

Easy Greens and Goat Cheese Lasagna

Lentil Stuffed Portobello Mushrooms

Mandarin Tofu Stir Fry

Baked Tortellini with Asparagus and Sun-Dried Tomatoes

Rice Noodles Primavera with Tofu and Peanut Sauce

Green Enchiladas

Greek Salad Wrap

THE FAMILY THAT EATS TOGETHER . . .

When I was growing up, my family ate dinner together every night. We sat at the table without any distractions. If the phone rang, it was pulled off the hook. In a huff, my mom would say, "Who could be calling at *dinnertime*?" The television was always off, and no one would even think to suggest watching TV while eating. We would not lift our forks until everyone was seated, and we would not leave until asking to be excused and saying, "Thank you for dinner." We didn't always love what we were served, but my brother and I respected the food and what went into making it.

With a two-year-old and a four-year-old, dinners at my house are not the way I remember them as an older child. Toddlers are far from civilized eaters. At any moment there is likely to be milk spilling onto the floor, a two-year-old climbing out of her highchair, or an overtired four-year-old crying because her pink fairy fork is in the dishwasher. Though dinnertime is often chaos with kids this young, I stick to the routine, because I know it is important for all of us and I know it will get easier. Even as toddlers, my kids now understand that there is one dinner made at dinnertime. They know that requests for other dishes will not be entertained, so they rarely ask.

One of the things I remember most from my teacher training in college is briefly learning the importance of family dinners. Having grown up with nightly family dinners, I thought nothing of it and had no idea just how beneficial eating together really is. Over the past few years studies have found that regular family dinners decrease depression in children and teens and the likelihood of kids trying drugs and alcohol and developing eating disorders. Children and teens who eat dinner with their families have better vocabularies, better grades, and higher self-esteem. They eat more vegetables and less fast food. In a 2011 study, the National Center on Addiction and

Substance Abuse at Columbia University (CASA) found that "compared to teens who have frequent family dinners (five to seven per week), those who have infrequent family dinners (fewer than three per week) are almost four times likelier to use tobacco; more than twice as likely to use alcohol; two and a half times likelier to use marijuana; and almost four times likelier to say they expect to try drugs in the future."

These statistics don't surprise me. We are all busy during the day and have to carve out quality time with our kids. If we don't sit down for dinner at the end of each day to really listen to our kids, then when do we do it? Eating dinner goes far beyond the food. It's a time we teach children table manners and shape their transition from food-throwing toddlers to civilized eaters. Dinnertime is a time kids can share how their day went and feel heard by their parents.

Between work, school, and after-school activities, finding time to make dinner is an obstacle. Cooking dinner at the end of a long day can seem like an overwhelmingly stressful task, but it doesn't have to be. Making dinner can be fun. When my little ones start getting cranky at five thirty, I plug my iPhone into a small speaker in the kitchen, turn on some music, and pour myself a small glass of wine. The girls and I dance to toddler music while we make dinner. This ritual is my favorite time of day, because cooking is a fun activity we do together. Getting kids involved in cooking their food makes them more likely to try it and to enjoy it, as they feel a sense of pride in the dinner they helped create. Even two-year-olds can sit on the floor and stir imaginary food with a whisk or line a muffin tin with wrappers. Cooking with kids is messy and does take longer than it might otherwise. However, after the mess is cleaned up, the joyful memories will remain.

Making quiche at home is much easier than most people think, and quiche is a great high-protein meatless meal for breakfast, lunch, or dinner. On nights when there seems to be nothing special in the fridge, I often make quiche, as I can always round up some eggs, cheese, milk, and vegetables. This quiche can be made hours ahead of time and reheated in a 300°F oven for 15 minutes. Feel free to replace the mushrooms and asparagus in this recipe with any vegetables you have on hand. Half a yellow onion or one whole shallot can be used if leeks are not available.

Mom's Best Quiche

1 prepared piecrust

1 tablespoon extra-virgin olive oil

1 leek, sliced

1 cup sliced cremini mushrooms

1 cup asparagus, cut into bite-size pieces

3 large eggs

½ cup heavy cream

1 cup milk

½ cup shredded Jarlsberg cheese

½ cup shredded Gruyère cheese

½ teaspoon Dijon mustard

Fresh cilantro, for garnish

Buying prepared piecrusts is easy, but there is nothing better than a flakey homemade butter piecrust. I use Martha Stewart's recipe that is made in a food processor. If you make your own piecrust, make a double batch and freeze half in plastic wrap.

Preheat the oven to 425°F. Roll out the piecrust dough and fit into a pie dish. Lightly poke the bottom and sides of the pastry all over with a fork. Line the dough with foil and fill with pie weights or dried beans. Bake for 15 minutes. Remove the weights and foil and continue baking another 5 minutes, or until the bottom is golden. Reduce the heat to 375°F.

Heat the olive oil in a skillet over medium-high heat. Add the leek, mushrooms, and asparagus to the pan. Add a pinch of salt and pepper and sauté the vegetables until softened, about 5 minutes. Transfer the vegetables to the crust with a slotted spoon, so that most of the liquid remains in the pan.

In a medium bowl, stir together the eggs, cream, milk, cheeses, and mustard. Pour the egg mixture over the vegetables. Bake for 50 minutes, until the quiche is firm and lightly browned. Check after 20 minutes to ensure that the crust is not browning too quickly. Cover the exposed crust with foil if it is getting too dark.

Serves 6 to 8

I created this recipe when my older daughter was just eighteen months old and loved black beans. Over three years later, this recipe has evolved from its original version and is still a favorite in our family. The kids love the sweet mango-avocado salsa packed into easy-to-hold pitas.

Black Bean Burgers with Mango-Avocado Salsa

1 medium mango, peeled and diced

1 small shallot, chopped

Juice of 1 lime

1 avocado, peeled, pitted, and diced

1 clove garlic, minced

¾ cup finely chopped fresh cilantro

¼ cup pomegranate seeds (optional)

2 (15-ounce) cans black beans, drained and rinsed

¾ cup shredded Monterey Jack cheese

¼ cup breadcrumbs

2 teaspoons ground cumin

1 teaspoon dried oregano

½ teaspoon sea salt

1 large egg, lightly beaten

3 pita bread pockets, halved

6 green leaf lettuce leaves

A nice dinner-time routine to get kids chatting is to ask the kids to share their favorite and least favorite parts of the day.

For the salsa, in a small bowl gently combine the mango, shallot, lime, avocado, garlic, ¼ cup cilantro, and the pomegranate seeds, if using.

Preheat the oven to 400°F. Coat a cookie sheet with cooking spray.

To make the burgers, in a medium bowl mash the beans with the back of a fork until all beans are broken and able to stick together, but still chunky. Stir in the remaining ½ cup cilantro, cheese, breadcrumbs, cumin, oregano, salt, and egg until combined. Form the mixture into 6 patties and place on the cookie sheet. Bake for 15 minutes, flipping the patties once.

Place one black bean patty, one leaf of lettuce, and some mango-avocado salsa into each half pita pocket.

Serves 6

The added cauliflower and tofu are barely noticeable and make this mac and cheese a meal complete with vegetables, protein, and carbohydrates.

Cauliflower Mac and Cheese

3 cups uncooked macaroni or other small pasta

3 cups cauliflower florets

2 tablespoons extra-virgin olive oil

2 tablespoons all-purpose flour

1 cup milk

1½ cups shredded sharp cheddar cheese

½ cup extra-firm tofu, crumbled

½ teaspoon salt

¼ teaspoon freshly cracked pepper

½ cup panko breadcrumbs

¼ cup grated Parmesan cheese

Time-saving tip: Mac and cheese is a perfect make-ahead meal. Assemble it in the morning or at naptime, store it in the refrigerator, and bake it in the evening. Make a double batch and freeze half before baking. This recipe can be frozen for up to three months when tightly sealed in plastic wrap and aluminum foil.

Preheat the oven to 375°F.

Bring a large pot of salted water to a boil. Add the pasta and cook according to package directions. When there are 3 minutes of cooking time left, add the cauliflower to pot and let it cook with pasta for the remaining time. Drain.

In another large pot, heat 1 tablespoon olive oil over medium heat. Whisk in the flour until smooth. Whisk in the milk, cooking until thickened, about 4 minutes. Remove from the heat and stir in the cheese, tofu, salt, pepper, cooked pasta, and cauliflower.

Transfer the mixture to 9 × 13-inch baking dish. Stir together the breadcrumbs, Parmesan, and remaining 1 tablespoon olive oil. Sprinkle over pasta. Bake for 30 minutes, or until breadcrumbs are golden brown.

Serves 6

For a long time take-out burritos were our family's go-to dinner of choice for busy nights. They are quick and inexpensive, but it wasn't long before we noticed we didn't feel well after take-out burrito nights. Now I create a quick veggie burrito bar filled with fresh ingredients and whole grains. Our burrito nights are healthier and tastier than ever—and just as quick as takeout. The kids love making their own burrito creations.

Fiesta Burritos

1 package flour or corn tortillas

15 ounces cooked or canned black beans, warmed up

2 cups cooked brown rice

1 red bell pepper, seeded and cut into strips

1 yellow bell pepper, seeded and cut into strips

1 large tomato, diced

½ cup crumbled queso fresco or other Mexican cheese

1 cup lettuce

1 small bunch fresh cilantro

1 cup Favorite Guacamole (recipe follows)

Warm the tortillas in a skillet over medium heat for 2 minutes. Transfer the tortillas to a plate. Place the beans, rice, peppers, tomato, cheese, lettuce, cilantro, and guacamole in individual serving bowls. Place on a lazy Susan or in the center of the table.

Serves 4

Favorite Guacamole

2 avocados, peeled and pitted
1 small onion, chopped
1 medium tomato, chopped
1 large clove garlic, minced
Juice of 1 lime
Salt and freshly cracked pepper to taste

Place all the ingredients in bowl and mash with a fork to desired consistency.

Makes about 2 cups

Sweet roasted butternut squash and sage are two of my favorite fall and winter flavors to put together. With its sweet squash and peas and savory herb pesto, this hearty pasta is a favorite with my kids and husband alike. To save time on a busy night, use precubed butternut squash and purchased pesto sauce with ½ cup fresh minced sage leaves stirred in.

Spaghetti with Roasted Butternut Squash, Peas, and Sage Pesto

1 medium butternut squash

2 tablespoons extra-virgin olive oil

½ teaspoon salt

1 pound spaghetti

½ cup sage pesto (recipe follows)

1 cup cooked peas

¼ cup shaved Parmesan cheese

¼ cup pine nuts, for garnish (optional)

¼ cup fresh basil or sage leaves, for garnish (optional)

Preheat the oven to 425°F. Using a vegetable peeler, peel the butternut squash. Cut in half crosswise, and then lengthwise. Scoop out and discard the seeds. Cut the squash into 1-inch cubes. Place on a large rimmed baking sheet. Drizzle with olive oil, sprinkle with salt, and toss to combine. Roast for 20 minutes until cooked through.

Bring a large pot of salted water to a boil. Add the spaghetti and cook until al dente, according to package directions. Drain, place in a bowl, and immediately toss with the pesto, peas, and roasted squash. Season to taste with salt and pepper. Top with shaved Parmesan. Garnish with pine nuts, fresh basil, or fresh sage, if desired.

Serves 6

Protein boost! Pancetta adds a wonderful smoky flavor to this recipe. Cook 4 ounces chopped pancetta in a pan over low heat for 5 minutes. Drain on a paper towel and add to pasta along with the vegetables. Shredded cooked chicken or sliced cooked sausage are also great add-ins. To keep the dish meat-less but increase the protein, use high-protein pasta, available at most supermarkets.

Sage Pesto

1½ cups packed fresh basil leaves
½ cup fresh sage leaves
2 cloves garlic, peeled
½ cup grated Parmesan cheese
¼ teaspoon freshly grated nutmeg
½ cup toasted pine nuts
⅓ cup extra-virgin olive oil
Salt and freshly cracked pepper to taste

Place the basil, sage, garlic, Parmesan, nutmeg, and pine nuts in the bowl of a food processor. Turn on and slowly pour the olive oil through feed tube. Process until all the ingredients are finely minced and combined. Season to taste with salt and pepper.

Makes about 1 cup

Double this recipe, or any sauce recipe, to save time later. Store half in a jar or freezer-safe container and freeze for up to three months.

My dad is famous for his calzone packed with garlic. Here is a recipe similar to the one my dad makes, but with a little less garlic and added spinach. Although Dad usually makes one large calzone and cuts it into slices, I like to make mini calzones that are easier for kids to hold.

Dad's Garlic Ricotta Calzone

Try making this calzone recipe with your own fillings. Simply add your favorites to the ricotta mixture before filling. Browned sausage, caramelized onions, sun-dried tomatoes, roasted peppers . . . the options are endless.

2 cups ricotta cheese

2 cups grated Asiago cheese, loosely packed

1 cup grated Parmesan cheese

1 large egg, beaten

5 cloves garlic, crushed

¼ cup chopped toasted pine nuts

1½ cups fresh basil, chopped

⅓ cup frozen spinach, thawed and drained

2 tablespoons extra-virgin olive oil

¼ teaspoon freshly cracked pepper

1 (16-ounce) prepared pizza dough, divided into 4 balls

Marinara sauce for dipping (optional; see Slow Cooker
    Veggie-Loaded Marinara, page 137)

Preheat the oven with a pizza stone to 550°F for 1 hour. Alternately, calzones can be baked on a cookie sheet lined with parchment paper.

In a medium bowl, stir together the ricotta, Asiago, Parmesan, egg, garlic, pine nuts, basil, spinach, olive oil, and pepper. Set aside.

Roll each ball of pizza dough into a circle about ⅛-inch thick and about 7½ inches in diameter. Place one-fourth of the filling on one half of each circle, leaving about ¾-inch border around the edge. Lightly wet the border with a little water. Bring the opposite side of dough over the filling and press to seal. Transfer to the pizza stone and bake for 7 to 10 minutes.

Serves 4 to 6

Pizza night doesn't have to mean a greasy unhealthy dinner. We have "pizza night" every couple of weeks, and the kids love decorating the pizza with toppings before I pop it into the oven. This rainbow pizza makes it especially fun for the kids to eat their veggies.

Summer Squash Rainbow Pizza

1 (16-ounce) prepared pizza dough

2 tablespoons extra-virgin olive oil

1 large clove garlic, minced

¼ cup shredded Italian cheese, such as mozzarella, Asiago, Parmesan, Fontina, or a blend

2 tablespoons crumbled feta cheese

1 zucchini, thinly sliced

1 yellow squash, thinly sliced

½ red onion, halved and thinly sliced

1 or 2 fresh Roma tomatoes, sliced

Coarse sea salt and freshly cracked pepper to taste

½ cup fresh basil leaves

Preheat the oven with a pizza stone to 550°F for 1 hour. Alternately, the pizza can be baked on a piece of parchment paper placed directly on the rack or on a cookie sheet.

In a small bowl, combine the olive oil and garlic. Roll out the pizza dough on a lightly floured piece of parchment paper until it's about ¼ inch thick. Brush the pizza dough with garlic olive oil. Sprinkle with the cheeses. Place the vegetables on pizza starting 1 inch from the outer edge and working inward in circles. Lightly brush veggies with garlic oil. Sprinkle with salt and pepper.

Transfer the pizza (with parchment, if using) to the pizza stone, oven rack, or cookie sheet. Bake for 8 to 10 minutes, until the crust has browned and the cheese has melted. Garnish with basil.

Serves 4 to 6

My mom makes the most delectable honey-curry glazed chicken breast. The sweet and savory sauce is mouthwatering. I took her sauce and turned it into an easy and filling vegan meal the whole family loves. Roasted vegetables and garbanzos with this sauce is one of my favorite easy weeknight dinners. Not only is it irresistibly yummy and healthy, the glaze, vegetables, and garbanzos are all made in one dish, making cleanup a snap!

Honey-Curry Glazed Vegetables and Garbanzos

Garbanzo beans (chickpeas) are a great source of filling protein and fiber, but alone they are an incomplete protein. However, the combination of garbanzos with nuts, seeds, or rice creates a complete protein, which is what our bodies need. This recipe is a healthy, complete meal all in one dish.

2 tablespoons butter or coconut oil

¼ cup honey

3 tablespoons Dijon mustard

2 teaspoons curry powder

½ teaspoon salt

5 cups cauliflower florets (about 1 large head)

5 carrots, cut into 1-inch pieces

1 (15-ounce) can garbanzo beans (chickpeas), drained and rinsed

2 tablespoons pepitas (pumpkin seeds) or pine nuts, for garnish

2 tablespoons fresh cilantro, for garnish

2 cups cooked quinoa or rice

Preheat the oven to 375°F.

Place butter in a 9 × 13-inch baking dish and place in oven just until the butter melts, about 2 minutes. Whisk the honey, Dijon mustard, curry powder, and salt into the butter to combine. Add the cauliflower florets, carrots, and garbanzo beans. Toss to coat the vegetables with the curry mixture. Bake uncovered for 30 to 35 minutes, until the vegetables are tender.

Garnish with pepitas and cilantro. Serve over quinoa or rice.

Serves 4

My husband loves eggplant, and especially Eggplant Parmesan. To avoid the fat and calories of this traditionally fried dish, I grill the eggplant and then roll the cheeses in the middle.

Grilled Eggplant Stuffed with Spinach and Cheese

2 tablespoons extra-virgin olive oil

2 cloves garlic, minced

1 (14.5-ounce) can crushed tomatoes

1 tablespoon tomato paste

1 teaspoon balsamic vinegar

¼ teaspoon salt

⅛ teaspoon freshly cracked pepper

¼ cup fresh basil leaves, chopped

1 globe eggplant, sliced lengthwise into long strips

1 cup ricotta cheese

¼ cup grated Parmesan cheese

¼ cup shredded mozzarella cheese

¼ cup frozen chopped spinach, thawed and drained

To make the tomato-basil sauce, heat 1 tablespoon of the oil in a medium saucepan over medium-low heat. Add the garlic and cook 1 minute, being careful not to burn it. Stir in the tomatoes, tomato paste, and balsamic vinegar and bring to a simmer. Season to taste with salt and pepper and simmer for 15 minutes. Stir in the basil. While the sauce is simmering, prepare the eggplant rolls.

To grill the eggplant, brush the strips with 1 tablespoon of olive oil and sprinkle with salt. Heat a grill pan over medium-high heat. Grill the eggplant in batches until softened, with dark grill marks, about 2 minutes per side. Remove from the heat.

Preheat the oven to 350°F. In a small bowl, stir together cheeses and spinach. Drop about 1½ tablespoons of the cheese mixture onto the center of each grilled eggplant slice and roll up. Spread the sauce on the bottom of an 8-inch square baking dish and place the eggplant rolls seam side down on top of the sauce. Bake uncovered for 20 minutes. Garnish with fresh basil.

Serves 4

I habitually get overly ambitious at the farmers' market and buy more than I can actually use in my recipes. At the end of the week I often end up with leftover vegetables. Letting good produce go bad is expensive and wasteful. My favorite solution to this problem is Farmers' Market Pasta. Any seasonal vegetables will work in this recipe. Have fun creating your own recipes. Try to include a variety of colors each time. Bulked up with vegetables, pasta can be a healthy meal—in stark contrast to many restaurant pastas. It's a great way to get kids to eat more vegetables and keep mummies in shape.

Farmers' Market Pasta

8 ounces pasta, any favorite shape

3 tablespoons extra-virgin olive oil

½ onion, chopped

2 cloves garlic, minced

1 teaspoon herbs of Provence

⅛ teaspoon salt

4 cups fresh seasonal vegetables cut into bite-size pieces

¼ cup dry white wine

Freshly cracked pepper to taste

¼ cup shaved Parmesan cheese

Boost the protein in this recipe by adding shredded cooked chicken breast, grilled shrimp, sliced salami, prosciutto, or meatless or traditional Italian sausage at the end.

Bring a large pot of salted water to a boil. Add the pasta and cook until al dente, according to package instructions. Reserve ¼ cup pasta water and drain.

Meanwhile, in a large skillet, heat the olive oil over medium-high heat. Sauté the onion until translucent, about 5 minutes. Stir in the garlic and continue to cook another minute. Stir in the herbs of Provence, salt, and vegetables. Add the firmest, densest vegetables first, as they will need to cook slightly longer. Add the white wine and cook until vegetables are tender-crisp. If there are hard vegetables, such as winter squash, broccoli, cauliflower, or Brussels sprouts, cover and cook 5 minutes, then cook uncovered for 2 minutes longer. If the vegetables are all softer varieties, such as zucchini, peas, tomatoes, or eggplant, leave the pan uncovered and cook for 5 minutes.

In a large bowl, toss the vegetables with the pasta. If the mixture is too dry, add pasta water until it is moist enough. Season to taste with salt and pepper. Top with Parmesan.

Serves 4

Southwestern Quinoa Stuffed Peppers

4 bell peppers, any color
1 ear of corn
1 cup cooked quinoa
1 cup canned black beans, drained and rinsed
1 cup cherry tomatoes, halved
¼ teaspoon salt
1 tablespoon chopped fresh cilantro
¼ cup shredded Monterey Jack cheese

Preheat the oven to 375°F.

Cut the tops off the peppers. With a spoon, gently scrape out the seeds
and ribs. Place the peppers in ½ inch of water in a large saucepan. Bring to
a simmer over medium-high heat, cover, and steam until the peppers are
tender-crisp, about 2 minutes. Remove the peppers and place cut side up
in an 8-inch square baking dish.

Place the corn in the same saucepan with water. Cover and steam until the
corn kernels can easily be pierced with a fork, about 6 minutes. Cool and
cut the kernels off of the cob.

In a medium bowl, stir together the quinoa, beans, tomatoes, salt, cilantro,
and corn. Spoon the quinoa mixture into the peppers. Sprinkle the cheese
over the top of the filling. Bake for 30 minutes, or until the cheese has
melted. Garnish with additional cilantro, if desired.

Serves 4

yummy mummy

LIFE TIP

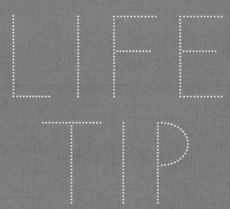

You can respect your children's tastes without allowing their dislikes to cause them to give up on an entire food group. If a child has tried a food and truly dislikes it, don't push the child to eat it. Pushing usually causes children to push back even harder. Allow children to have one or two foods they do not have to eat. In our family, one child does not like cheese. Cheese can have a strong flavor, and I can understand her dislike of it, so I don't force her to eat it. Without any pressure, she's starting to try some cheeses and beginning to enjoy them.

Spaghetti squash is a fun vegetable for kids to help make. The interior of the hard squash turns into strands of "spaghetti" after it's baked. Have kids help scrape out the "spaghetti." This recipe is perfect for anyone avoiding wheat.

Baked Spaghetti Squash and "Meatballs"

1 large spaghetti squash
1 (16-ounce) batch meatless meatballs
1 cup marinara or spaghetti sauce (see Slow Cooker Veggie-Loaded Marinara, page 137)
½ cup shredded mozzarella cheese
½ cup grated Parmesan cheese
1 cup fresh basil leaves, torn or sliced

Preheat the oven to 375°F.

Cut the squash in half lengthwise. Scoop out the seeds. Brush or drizzle with olive oil. Place on a baking sheet, cut side down, and bake for 30 to 40 minutes. Cool slightly on the baking sheet. Turn the oven up to 400°F.

Using a fork, scrape squash "spaghetti" up from the rind and fluff into strands. Place meatballs over squash. Pour the sauce over the meatballs and "spaghetti." Sprinkle the cheeses over the sauce. Bake the stuffed squash halves on a cookie sheet until the cheese is melted and bubbling. Top with fresh basil and serve right out of the squash.

Serves 4 to 6

Meatless meat-balls are available at Trader Joe's and Whole Foods.

You've heard it said that the best spaghetti sauces are simmered all afternoon. If that's true, why not let the slow cooker do the cooking for you? This sauce takes 5 minutes to make and is loaded with vitamins. Make a double batch and freeze half for another day.

Slow Cooker Veggie-Loaded Marinara

2 carrots, chopped

2 celery stalks, chopped

1 yellow onion, chopped

1 red bell pepper, chopped

2 large cloves garlic, minced

2 (28-ounce) containers whole peeled tomatoes,
    drained and crushed with your hands

2 tablespoons tomato paste

1 bay leaf

1 teaspoon dried oregano

½ cup fresh basil, chopped

½ teaspoon salt

⅛ teaspoon freshly cracked pepper

Combine all the ingredients in slow cooker and cook on low for 6 hours. Remove the bay leaf. Blend with an immersion blender to the desired consistency. Adjust the seasonings to taste.

Makes about 6 cups

Don't chop vegetables while holding a baby! I use a food processor to quickly chop onions and other vegetables when I only have one hand free. A food processor has a permanent place on my kitchen counter for this reason.

This recipe has become a favorite among my mommy friends for its ease of preparation and big kid-friendly dose of veggies. I adapt the recipe seasonally, using zucchini in the summer and Brussels sprouts in the winter.

Easy Greens and Goat Cheese Lasagna

2 tablespoons extra-virgin olive oil

1 leek, halved lengthwise and sliced crosswise into ¼-inch
    pieces

1 bunch asparagus, cut into 1-inch pieces

1 cup chopped zucchini

5 ounces fresh baby spinach

15 ounces ricotta cheese

5 ounces goat cheese, at room temperature

1 large egg, lightly beaten

4 ounces pesto

1 package no-boil or fresh lasagna noodles

½ cup shredded Italian cheese, such as mozzarella,
    Parmesan, Asiago, or a blend

½ cup fresh basil, for garnish (optional)

Preheat the oven to 350°F.

Heat the oil in a large saucepan over medium heat. Add the leeks, asparagus, and zucchini. Season with salt and pepper. Cook until the vegetables are tender-crisp, 3 to 4 minutes. Stir in the spinach until wilted, about 2 minutes. Remove from the heat.

In a medium bowl, stir together the ricotta, goat cheese, and egg. Season with salt and pepper.

Spread a thin layer of pesto over the bottom of an 11 × 7-inch casserole dish. (A 9 × 13-inch dish would work too, but I prefer the 11 × 7 for this recipe.) Place a layer of lasagna noodles over the pesto. Spoon half of the vegetable mixture over the noodles. Spread half of the ricotta mixture over the vegetables. Top the ricotta layer with a second layer of noodles, then the rest of the pesto, the rest of the vegetables, and the rest of the ricotta mixture. Sprinkle the shredded Italian cheese over the top. Bake for 40 minutes, or until noodles are cooked through. If the cheese begins to brown too quickly, cover with foil. Let cool 10 minutes before serving. Garnish with basil, if desired.

Serves 6

Mushrooms offer a meatiness that is great for vegetarian dishes like this one. Lentils add protein and fiber. I like to use mini portobello mushrooms, which are perfect for little hands. With a sprinkle of Parmesan, these healthy vegetable-filled cups taste almost like pizza.

Lentil Stuffed Portobello Mushrooms

2 tablespoons extra-virgin olive oil

1 small onion, chopped

2 carrots, chopped

1 celery stalk, chopped

2 cloves garlic, minced

1 teaspoon herbs of Provence; or mixture of rosemary, thyme, lavender, and fennel seed; or fresh herbs

2 cups cooked lentils

Salt and freshly cracked pepper to taste

4 large portobello mushrooms (or 8 or more smaller portobellos), center stalks removed

2 tablespoons grated Parmesan cheese

Fresh herbs, for garnish

Heat 1 tablespoon of the oil over medium heat in a large sauté pan. Cook the onion, carrots, celery, garlic, and herbs until the vegetables are tender. Stir in the lentils and season to taste with salt and pepper. Transfer the lentil-vegetable mixture to a large bowl.

Wipe the pan clean, add the other tablespoon of olive oil, and cook the mushrooms for about 2 minutes per side until starting to soften. Place the mushrooms, cap down, in a baking dish. Fill the mushrooms with the lentil mixture. Drizzle with a little olive oil on top if dry. Sprinkle with Parmesan. Place under the broiler until warm and the cheese starts to melt, about 2 minutes. Transfer to a serving plate and garnish with fresh herbs such as parsley or basil.

Serves 4

Mandarin Tofu Stir Fry

2 tablespoons orange juice

2 tablespoons soy sauce

1 tablespoon maple syrup

1 large clove garlic, minced

1 teaspoon freshly grated ginger

2 tablespoons sesame or vegetable oil

2 carrots

4 ounces broccolini

1 baby bok choy

1 red bell pepper

½ red onion

1 cup sugar snap peas

8 ounces extra-firm tofu

1 (11-ounce) can mandarin oranges, drained

4 cups cooked jasmine rice

For the sauce, in a small bowl, whisk together the orange juice, soy sauce, syrup, garlic, and ginger.

Cut the carrots, broccolini, bok choy, bell pepper, onion, snap peas, and tofu into bite-size pieces. Heat the oil in a wok or large pan over high heat. When the oil starts to sizzle, add all the vegetables. Stir and cook until tender-crisp, about 4 minutes. Add the sauce to the pan and continue to cook for another 2 minutes. Remove from the heat. Gently stir in the oranges.

Serve over rice with additional soy sauce, if desired.

Serves 4

Don't underestimate the importance of spending quality time with your kids. While her friends were leaving the children with nannies, Tai Tai played with her kids at the beach and brought them along on trips all over the world. Over fifty years later, her children still remember and appreciate those special times.

Baked Tortellini with Asparagus and Sun-Dried Tomatoes

2 tablespoons extra-virgin olive oil

1 bunch asparagus, cut into 1½-inch pieces

½ onion, chopped

2 cloves garlic, minced

1 (14.5-ounce) can crushed tomatoes

1 teaspoon chopped fresh parsley

¼ teaspoon salt

¼ teaspoon freshly cracked pepper

10 ounces cheese tortellini

¼ cup sun-dried tomatoes

1 cup shredded mozzarella cheese

½ cup grated Parmesan cheese

¼ cup fresh basil leaves, for garnish

Preheat the oven to 375°F.

Heat the olive oil in a saucepan over medium-high heat. Add the asparagus and cook until tender-crisp, about 4 to 5 minutes. Remove the asparagus from the pan. Add the onion to the same pan and sauté until translucent, about 5 minutes. Add the garlic and sauté another minute longer. Stir in tomatoes, parsley, salt, and pepper. Simmer, stirring occasionally, until sauce has thickened, about 10 minutes. Remove from the heat.

Meanwhile, bring a large pot of salted water to a boil. Add the tortellini and cook until al dente, according to package directions, about 3 minutes.

Drain the tortellini and add to the sauce. Stir in the asparagus, sun-dried tomatoes, ½ cup mozzarella, and ¼ cup Parmesan. Pour the pasta mixture into a 9 × 13-inch baking dish. Sprinkle with the remaining ½ cup mozzarella and ¼ cup Parmesan and bake until cheese has melted, about 15 to 20 minutes. Garnish with basil.

Serves 4

Beautiful strands of carrots and zucchini intertwine with rice noodles, adding color, flavor, and nutrients. A sweet and savory peanut sauce coats the vegetables, tofu, and noodles. Kids can help by whisking together the sauce ingredients, and older kids can even julienne the vegetables with the help of an adult. I like to use a julienne peeler made by Swissmar available at Williams-Sonoma.

Rice Noodles Primavera with Tofu and Peanut Sauce

2 tablespoons peanut oil

1 clove garlic, minced

1 tablespoon grated fresh ginger

⅔ cup creamy natural peanut butter

2 tablespoons hot water

3 tablespoons soy sauce

1 tablespoon honey

10 ounces rice noodles

3 large carrots, julienned with a mandolin or peeler

1 large zucchini, julienned with a mandolin or peeler

1 cup sugar snap peas

7 ounces baked tofu, cubed

¼ cup chopped peanuts

¼ cup sliced green onions

Pea tendrils and flowers, for garnish (optional)

Many herbs, fruits, and vegetables have beautiful edible flowers. An added bonus for growing your own is getting to decorate your dishes with flowers. Even small potted herbs on a windowsill can yield dainty decorative flowers. Rosemary and thyme, for example, have tiny purple flowers, and basil has white ones.

For the sauce, in a small bowl, whisk together the peanut oil, garlic, ginger, peanut butter, water, soy sauce, and honey. Set aside.

Bring 4 quarts of water to a boil. Add the noodles and cook for 4 minutes. Add the carrots, zucchini, and sugar snap peas to the boiling water and cook 1 minute longer. Drain.

Transfer the noodles and vegetables to a large serving bowl. Stir in the tofu and sauce. Top with peanuts and green onions. Garnish with pea tendrils and flowers, if desired.

Serves 4

Everyone loves enchiladas. I couldn't find a recipe I liked for meatless enchiladas until I came up with this one. It's hearty and filling, and no one will even miss the meat.

Green Enchiladas

1 tablespoon extra-virgin olive oil

5 ounces fresh baby spinach

1 (15-ounce) can black beans, rinsed and drained

½ cup cooked brown rice

1½ cups sliced cremini mushrooms

¼ cup chopped fresh cilantro

2 ounces goat cheese, crumbled

2 cups mild tomatillo green salsa, fresh or jarred

½ cup half and half

6 (9-inch) flour or brown-rice tortillas

1 cup shredded Mexican cheese, Monterey Jack, cheddar, Colby, or a blend

1 avocado, chopped, for garnish

¼ cup fresh cilantro leaves

1 lime, cut into wedges

Preheat the oven to 375°F.

Heat the oil in a large skillet over medium heat. Add the spinach and toss until just wilted. Remove from the heat and transfer the spinach to a medium bowl. To the spinach add the beans, rice, mushrooms, cilantro, and goat cheese. Gently toss to combine.

In another medium bowl, stir together the salsa and half and half. Pour half of the salsa mixture into an 11 × 7-inch baking dish. Fill the tortillas with 1 cup of filling each and roll up. Place the filled tortillas seam side down in the baking dish. Pour the remaining half of the salsa mixture over the enchiladas. Sprinkle with cheese. Bake uncovered for 25 to 30 minutes. Cool slightly. Garnish with avocado, cilantro, and lime.

Serves 4 to 6

Wraps make an easy, healthy lunch. Here the hummus acts as a "glue" holding the wrap together. My little preschooler loves this wrap in her lunchbox. I make a whole wrap in the morning and send half to school with her and keep the other half in the fridge for me. I have also cut these wraps into 2-inch pieces and served them at play dates and birthday parties.

Greek Salad Wrap

1 piece lavash bread or large tortilla

2 tablespoons hummus

½ cup fresh baby spinach or lettuce

¼ cup halved cherry tomatoes

¼ cup sliced and halved English hothouse or
    Persian cucumber

2 tablespoons canned garbanzo beans

1 tablespoon crumbled feta cheese

1 tablespoon favorite salad dressing

Spread the hummus over the lavash. Place the lettuce, tomatoes, cucumber, garbanzo beans, and feta on one short side of the lavash. Drizzle with dressing. Roll the wrap tightly from the short side. Cut in half crosswise.

Makes 2 small or 1 large wrap

Wraps are great for quick, healthy lunches—and the filling combinations are endless. Keep a package of lavash and a container of hummus in your fridge and find out which wrap combinations your kids like best. Guacamole (see Favorite Guacamole, page 115) makes another great "glue" for vegetable wraps with beans and rice.

from the sea

Potato-Scaled Halibut

Macadamia-Crusted Mahi Mahi with Mango Couscous

15-Minute Mascarpone Fettuccine with Broiled Salmon

Halibut with Blood Orange Salsa

Mediterranean Orzo with Seared Scallops

Pineapple Mojito Tilapia

Crispy Baked "Fish and Chips"

Grilled Tilapia Gyros

Baked Salmon with Lemon-Artichoke Pesto

Lobster Tacos with Kumquats and Avocado-Cilantro Sauce

Make-Ahead Tilapia and Asparagus Baked in Parchment

FISH: A MOSTLY MEATLESS FAMILY'S BEST FRIEND

I have always been drawn to the ocean. Even though I have lived on the coast my entire life, whenever I travel to other parts of the world, I am intrigued by fishermen and seafood. They give a peek into the culture and feeling of a seaside town. On the coast of Italy the colorful little fishing boats dotting the azure sea or docked just yards from cafés loll sleepily on the waves and allude to a slower-paced lifestyle. Throughout the Greek Islands similar boats—each with a sleeping cat lying on a warm deck—all leave me daydreaming about the sun-drenched fishing adventures that must take place there. The Venetian fishermen and chefs, so proud of their famous black squid-ink spaghetti, are captivating. Here in California there is an abundance of fresh seafood too. Every Sunday in Santa Barbara fishermen bring their fresh catch of the morning to the harbor to sell. Visiting the fishermen's market is always a fun and refreshing experience for our family. Just as I am, the girls are curious to see what has been caught just offshore.

While visiting friends in Hawaii as a young woman, I watched a fisherman pull a swordfish into a boat in the afternoon and my friends grill it and place it on the dinner table a few hours later. I was fifteen years old, and I can still remember how wonderful that fresh swordfish tasted. Not a trace of fishiness could be detected. This fish, simply grilled with a little salt, pepper, and olive oil, conjured up the tropical breezes at the beach. It was then that I fell in love with fish.

Years later I ended up marrying the most wonderful man. Unfortunately he did not like fish. Phil said he found the fishy taste disgusting. I agreed, fishiness is not a pleasant taste. However, I knew he just hadn't been eating the right fish, and I set out to change his mind about my favorite food. I started by occasionally serving a very fresh mild local fish like halibut for dinner. To his surprise, Phil exclaimed, "This is really good. It's not fishy at all. I like halibut!" The secret to fish that doesn't taste fishy is to buy it as fresh as possible. Fish is perfect for busy moms, as it cooks quickly. Many of the recipes in this chapter can be on the table within 20 minutes. Making fish for the family doesn't have to mean bland fish sticks. For those who don't think they like fish, I add more flavors or textures. Phil devoured my Macadamia-Crusted Mahi Mahi with Mango Couscous (page 160) as if he were a seasoned fish lover. The crunchy crust and tropical flavor are enough to entice any self-proclaimed fish hater.

Fish is a great source of high-quality protein. It contains omega–3 fatty acids, which are important for several health reasons, including proper eye and brain development. The American Heart Association recommends eating fish, especially fatty fish such as salmon, at least twice a week for the omega–3 heart-health benefits. When you are cutting down on chicken, beef, and pork, fish can be a healthy alternative. In our family seafood is a significant protein source, as we avoid other meats as much as possible. A dinner of lean fish and vegetables is a favorite of mine and many of my mummy friends, because it helps us look and feel great. The recipes in this chapter will help you create easy and elegant seafood dinners that kids, moms, and even husbands who don't like fish will love. A great place to start is with 15-Minute Mascarpone Fettuccine with Broiled Salmon (page 162), as kids are drawn to the creamy pasta.

With fish, you can illustrate to kids where our food comes from by taking them to the ocean. Take your kids fishing or to a harbor to see fish coming out of the water. Bring that fresh fish home and cook and taste it with your kids. Kids are fascinated by the underwater world and love getting a glimpse of it through seafood.

My favorite seafood dish is Potato-Scaled Mahi Mahi from Nick's Fishmarket on Maui. Potato "fish scales" create a crunchy crust on the flaky white fish. Nick's serves its potato-scaled fish on a potato puree with a cabernet sauce and white truffle oil. I've simplified this idea into an easy dinner to make at home. I most often use halibut because we have it locally, but any firm white fish can be used.

Potato-Scaled Halibut

4 (6-ounce) halibut fillets
Salt and freshly cracked pepper to taste
5 baby red potatoes, sliced paper-thin
1 tablespoon extra-virgin olive oil

Preheat a broiler pan at the top of the oven. Season the fish lightly with salt and pepper. Lay the potato slices over the top of the fish, overlapping slightly. Drizzle with olive oil. Sprinkle the top of the potatoes with salt.

Broil for 7 to 10 minutes until the potatoes have browned and the fish flakes easily. Watch closely to make sure the potatoes don't burn. If the potatoes are browning too quickly, move the pan lower in the oven or cover with foil.

Serves 4

I love fish dishes that make me feel as though I'm on a tropical vacation, and this recipe does just that. I love the sweet, colorful mango couscous with the crunchy tropical fish. Store-bought mango salsa makes this meal incredibly quick and easy to prepare.

Macadamia-Crusted Mahi Mahi with Mango Couscous

4 (6-ounce) mahi mahi fillets

Salt and freshly cracked pepper to taste

1 cup macadamia nuts

½ cup flaked coconut

2 tablespoons all-purpose flour

2 large eggs

2 tablespoons vegetable oil

1 cup uncooked couscous

14-ounce container fresh mango salsa

Create your own tropical vacation by turning on some Hawaiian music and hula dancing with your kids while you make this dish. Serve virgin piña coladas topped with tiny umbrellas for dessert.

Season the fish with salt and pepper. In a food processor, pulse the nuts, coconut, and flour until the nuts are coarsely chopped. Transfer the nut mixture to a large shallow bowl. In another large shallow bowl, beat the eggs with a whisk. Dip each fillet into the egg to coat it, let the excess drip off, and place it in the nut mixture, turning to coat.

In a large skillet, heat the oil over medium-high heat. Add the fish and cook until lightly browned and cooked through, about 3 minutes per side. Remove and place on paper towels to absorb excess oil.

Meanwhile, cook couscous according to the package directions.

In a medium bowl, stir together salsa and couscous. Spoon the mango couscous onto plates and top with the fish.

Serves 4

Creamy mascarpone pasta makes this fish kid-friendly, while remaining elegant. Microgreens on top add a fresh finishing touch, but are optional. Microgreens are tiny baby lettuces and herbs that can add fresh flavor and color to salads and other dishes. They are now available at most grocery stores, including Trader Joe's and Whole Foods.

15-Minute Mascarpone Fettuccine with Broiled Salmon

8 ounces fresh or dried fettuccine

¾ pound wild salmon

1 tablespoon extra-virgin olive oil

1 cup whole milk

1 clove garlic, minced

½ cup grated Parmesan cheese

6 ounces mascarpone cheese

Salt and freshly cracked pepper to taste

1 tablespoon chopped fresh parsley, for garnish

1 cup microgreens, for garnish

For the pasta, bring a large pot of salted water to a boil. Add the fettuccine and cook until al dente, according to package directions.

For the salmon, preheat the broiler. Brush the salmon with olive oil and sprinkle with salt and pepper. Broil the salmon until it reaches the desired doneness, 5 to 10 minutes. Cut the salmon into 2-inch pieces.

For the sauce, in a large pot over medium-low heat, bring the milk and garlic to a simmer. Stir in the Parmesan and mascarpone. Season with salt and pepper. Remove from the heat and stir in the cooked pasta. Pour the sauced pasta into a serving bowl and top with the salmon. Garnish with chopped parsley and microgreens.

Serves 4

LIFE TIP

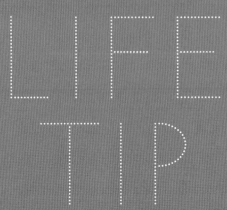

I choose wild salmon whenever possible. Many, but not all, farmed salmon are raised in dirty crowded pens and are not sustainable. Farmed salmon has been shown to have high levels of PCBs (polychlorinated biphenyls). PCBs are artificial chemicals believed to increase the risk of cancer, among other health concerns.

Navigating the varieties of fish now that there are health worries over pollutants can be confusing. Thankfully, online organizations can help, like Seafood Watch from the Monterey Bay Aquarium. Fishmongers are often very knowledgeable and can provide information, and some stores, like Whole Foods, display sustainability ratings in their fish departments.

Halibut with Blood Orange Salsa

2 blood oranges
1 tangerine
1 clove garlic, minced
1 small shallot, chopped
1 tablespoon chopped fresh cilantro
Juice of 1 lime
4 (6-ounce) halibut fillets
Extra-virgin olive oil
Salt and freshly cracked pepper to taste

For the salsa, peel and roughly chop the oranges and tangerine. Place in a small bowl and add the garlic, shallot, cilantro, and lime juice. Stir to combine.

Heat a grill or grill pan to high heat. Brush the fish with olive oil and season with salt and pepper. Place the fish on the grill and cook until it flakes easily, about 3 minutes per side. Remove from the heat and serve with the blood orange salsa.

Serves 4

Halibut is my favorite fish. It has a mild flavor that is palatable for those who don't think they like fish.

Orzo is such a comforting food. Tossed with a little olive oil, it was one of the first foods I fed my girls. My favorite way to serve orzo now that my girls are a little older is filled with fresh colorful vegetables like sweet bell pepper, tomatoes, and arugula. Topped with scallops, this Mediterranean-inspired orzo dish is a healthy, complete meal.

Mediterranean Orzo with Seared Scallops

1½ cups uncooked orzo
4 tablespoons extra-virgin olive oil
Juice of ½ lemon
1 tablespoon chopped fresh oregano
1 teaspoon chopped fresh thyme
1 cup cherry tomatoes, halved
1 yellow or orange bell pepper, seeded and diced
½ cup Greek olives, such as Kalamata, pitted for small children
2 cups arugula leaves
Salt and freshly cracked pepper to taste
16 jumbo scallops

Bring a large pot of salted water to a boil. Add the orzo and cook until al dente, about 9 minutes. Reserve ¼ cup of the pasta water and drain the orzo. In a large bowl, toss the orzo with 3 tablespoons olive oil, lemon juice, oregano, thyme, tomatoes, bell pepper, olives, and arugula. Season to taste with salt and pepper. If the pasta is too dry, add pasta water by the tablespoon until it reaches the right consistency.

Meanwhile, heat 1 tablespoon of olive oil in nonstick frying pan over high heat. Sprinkle scallops with salt and pepper. Cook scallops 3 minutes per side. Top the orzo with the scallops. Garnish with any extra fresh thyme or oregano.

Serves 4

This recipe was inspired by one of my favorite cocktails—the mojito. The flavors are just as delicious and fun on top of a piece of white fish. Tilapia is a great seafood choice, because it is not only mild tasting, but sustainable, healthy, and inexpensive.

Pineapple Mojito Tilapia

1¼ cups fresh pineapple chunks
1 shallot
¼ cup fresh cilantro, loosely packed
2 tablespoons fresh mint, loosely packed
Juice of 1 lime
1 tablespoon rum
¼ cup pineapple juice
1 pound tilapia fillets

Kids can enjoy this recipe too! The alcohol burns off with cooking, but the flavor remains. If you are concerned about the alcohol in any of these recipes, simply omit it.

In the bowl of a food processor pulse the pineapple, shallot, cilantro, mint, and lime juice until the pineapple and shallot are as roughly chopped as they would be in a salsa. Transfer all but 2 tablespoons of the pineapple mixture to a small bowl. To the remaining pineapple mixture, add the rum and pineapple juice. Pulse 2 seconds to combine.

Place the tilapia in a shallow dish and cover with the pineapple juice mixture. Let marinate for 15 minutes. Coat a grill or grill pan with cooking spray and heat to medium-high heat. Remove the tilapia and discard the marinade. Place the tilapia on the grill and cook until done, about 3 minutes per side. Serve with the reserved pineapple topping.

Serves 4

Crispy Baked "Fish and Chips"

1 tablespoon extra-virgin olive oil, plus 1 teaspoon

1 pound tilapia or halibut fillets

1 large egg

1 cup panko breadcrumbs

1 teaspoon chopped fresh parsley

½ teaspoon salt

⅛ teaspoon freshly cracked pepper

3 russet potatoes

To prepare the fish, preheat the oven to 450°F. Brush a baking sheet with 1 tablespoon of olive oil. Cut the fish into approximately 4 × 2-inch pieces. Whisk the egg in a medium-size shallow dish. In another medium-size shallow dish, stir together the breadcrumbs, parsley, ¼ teaspoon salt, and pepper. Dip each piece of fish into the egg and turn to coat. Remove, let the excess drip off, then place in the breadcrumb mixture, and turn to coat. Place the fish pieces on the prepared baking sheet.

For the "chips," cut the potatoes into about ½-inch-wide "fries." Toss with 1 teaspoon olive oil and ¼ teaspoon salt. Place on the pan with the fish or on a separate pan. Bake the fish and potatoes for about 15 minutes, depending on the thickness, turning once, until browned and cooked through.

Serves 4

Grilled Tilapia Gyros

¾ cup plain low-fat Greek yogurt

2 teaspoons chopped fresh dill

1½ teaspoons fresh lemon juice

¼ Persian cucumber, sliced paper-thin

¼ teaspoon salt

½ teaspoon freshly cracked pepper

2 cloves garlic, minced

1 pound tilapia fillets

1 tablespoon extra-virgin olive oil

Salt and freshly cracked pepper to taste

4 flatbreads

1 medium tomato, thinly sliced

¾ Persian cucumber, thinly sliced

½ cup fresh baby spinach

1 avocado, thinly sliced

For the tzatziki sauce, stir together the yogurt, dill, lemon juice, cucumber, salt, pepper, and garlic in a small bowl. Set aside, or refrigerate if made in advance.

For the fish, preheat a grill or grill pan to medium-high heat. Brush the tilapia with olive oil and season with salt and pepper. Grill the fish until cooked through, about 3 minutes per side.

Spread about 2 tablespoons tzatziki sauce on one side of each flatbread. Place one-fourth of the tilapia on top of the sauce on each. Divide the tomato, cucumber, spinach, and avocado and place evenly on top of the tilapia; fold the flatbreads over.

Serves 4

Rich salmon is brightened up with fresh lemon slices and an artichoke pesto featuring a handful of fresh basil leaves.

Baked Salmon with Lemon-Artichoke Pesto

1 cup fresh basil leaves

3 cloves garlic

¼ cup pine nuts

¼ teaspoon salt

⅛ teaspoon freshly cracked pepper

Juice of ½ lemon

2 tablespoons extra-virgin olive oil

1 (8.5-ounce) can artichoke hearts in water

1 pound wild salmon fillets

1 lemon, thinly sliced

Completely assemble this recipe up to 8 hours in advance. Cover with foil and refrigerate until you're ready to bake it for dinner. My mom and I like to make this recipe for stress-free entertaining. This dish is almost done long before guests even arrive and is much easier than it looks or tastes.

Preheat the oven to 375°F.

Place the basil, garlic, pine nuts, salt, pepper, and lemon juice in the bowl of a food processor. Pulse until all the ingredients are finely chopped. Add the olive oil and continue to pulse until combined. Reserve ⅓ cup artichoke hearts, and place the rest into the food processor with the basil mixture. Pulse until the artichokes are roughly chopped and combined.

Place the salmon in a baking dish. Spread the artichoke pesto over the salmon. Cut the reserved ⅓ cup of artichoke hearts into quarters. Top the artichoke pesto–covered salmon with lemon slices and quartered artichoke hearts. Cover with foil and bake for about 40 minutes, until the salmon easily flakes with a fork.

Serves 4

Indulging in lobster always makes the occasion feel special. Though it's expensive, a little can go a long way when made in dishes like lobster risotto, lobster mac and cheese, and here in tacos.

Lobster Tacos with Kumquats and Avocado-Cilantro Sauce

3 tablespoons sour cream or crème fraiche

Juice and zest of 1 lime

¼ cup fresh cilantro, plus 2 sprigs for garnish

½ avocado, peeled, halved, and pitted

½ teaspoon salt

2 lobster tails in shells

2 tablespoons extra-virgin olive oil

4 corn tortillas

1 cup shredded cabbage

¼ cup kumquats, thinly sliced crosswise

¼ teaspoon coarse sea salt

To make the avocado-cilantro sauce, place the sour cream, lime juice and zest, ¼ cup cilantro, avocado, and salt in the bowl of a food processor. Pulse until combined and smooth. Transfer to a small bowl, cover, and refrigerate until ready to use.

To prepare the lobster, heat the grill to medium-high. Using a large sharp knife, cut the lobster tails in half lengthwise. Brush with olive oil. Place the lobster tails cut side down on the hot grill and cook for 4 to 5 minutes, until grill marks can be seen. Flip the lobster over and continue to cook another 4 minutes, until cooked through. Remove from the grill and let rest until cool enough to handle. Remove the lobster meat from the shell and cut into bite-size pieces.

Warm the tortillas by placing them on the grill for 1 minute. Place ¼ cup of shredded cabbage on each tortilla. Top with about 1 tablespoon avocado-cilantro sauce. Divide the lobster meat and kumquats evenly and place on top of cabbage and sauce. Finish with a pinch of sea salt. Garnish with cilantro.

Makes 4 tacos

yummy mummy

LIFE TIP

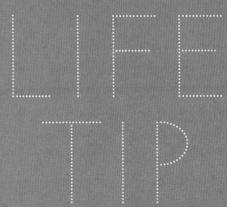

You don't have to wait for a special occasion to enjoy finer things like lobster. Any day is a good day to pull out the good crystal glasses and have a sip of champagne.

Steaming fish in parchment-paper packages is a healthy and simple way to make a juicy dish. Packages can be prepared early in the day and kept in the refrigerator until dinnertime. Baking fish "en papillote" has the added bonus of using no cooking dishes, which means very little cleanup.

Make-Ahead Tilapia and Asparagus Baked in Parchment

1 small bunch asparagus
1 tablespoon extra-virgin olive oil
1 pound tilapia fillets
1 lemon, thinly sliced
4 sprigs fresh oregano
4 sprigs fresh thyme
Salt and freshly cracked pepper to taste

Preheat the oven to 400°F. Tear off four (15 × 24-inch) pieces of parchment paper. Fold each piece in half.

Snap the tough ends off the asparagus. Drizzle the asparagus and fish with olive oil and sprinkle with a pinch of salt and pepper.

Open the parchment pieces and place four asparagus spears on one side of the paper. Place one-fourth of the tilapia directly on top of the asparagus on each paper. Top the fish with one sprig of thyme and one sprig of oregano. Place two lemon slices over the herbs. Wrap the other side of parchment over the fish. Twist the two edges of parchment together to seal the packages. Place parchment packages on a cookie sheet and bake for 15 minutes.

Serves 4

Plan some of your dinner-making time during the day to avoid the last-minute scramble to get dinner on the table in the evening. I find it easiest to get as much cooking prep done as possible while younger kids are napping.

desserts

Apricot Almond Crumble Bars

Mini Ice Cream Pies

Broiled Peach and Biscotti Parfaits

Lavender Cupcakes

Pomegranate Chocolate Chunk Sherbet

Salted Brown Butter Cookies

Chocolate Hazelnut Shortbread

Fudgy Pinwheel Cookies

Healthy Raspberry-Apple Crisp with Coconut-Oat Topping

Strawberry Lemonade Tiramisu

Grandma's Lemon Angel Pie

Berry Shortcake

Caramelized Banana Split Crepes

Frozen Scottish Raspberry Soufflé

Pumpkin and Chocolate Mousse Trifle

JUST ONE SQUARE

Between the ages of five and ten, I used to occasionally have sleepovers at my grand-mother's house. I loved sleeping in her tall, fluffy hotel-like bed, listening to the train go by, and hearing the booming gong of the grandfather clock echoing off the cool hardwood floors. What tickled me most about staying at grandma's house, though, was the chocolate bar by the bed. Grandma has always kept a bar of Cadbury's chocolate with fruit and nuts on her nightstand. Every night she has just one square of chocolate. I remember giggling to myself, thinking it was so silly that an old lady would keep chocolate by her bed.

Tai Tai has always been very health conscious and maintained a svelte figure, but allows herself little indulgences rather than denying herself the foods she loves. Most nights she has a little dessert after dinner, most likely a scoop of coffee Häagen-Dazs ice cream. My mom has followed Tai Tai's example and treats herself to a tiny bit of good-quality chocolate every day. Mom keeps a jar of chocolate-covered almonds in her office drawer and has just one or two when she craves a sweet treat. Though I have less self-control when it comes to desserts, I try to stick to this philosophy, which has worked so well for the Yummy Mummies before me. I don't believe one has to deprive oneself of anything to maintain a healthy lifestyle. The key is moderation. Eat-ing healthfully most of the time allows for a little indulgence, as long as it's "just one square" or just for special occasions.

I love making beautiful decadent desserts. They make any day more special. Kids remember the cupcakes from their birthday parties. I clearly remember the mouse-shaped cake with licorice whiskers my mom baked for my fourth birthday party in the park. Adults remember the stunning desserts that are the highlight of a dinner party. It makes me happy to create a beautifully decorated batch of cupcakes and watch faces light up at the sight of them. Sweet treats made with love are a way to show people that you care. A warm cookie from the oven can brighten anyone's day. There's nothing better than a gooey chocolate chip oozing from a cookie fresh from the oven. I love baking cookies with my girls on rainy days. The girls are eager to mix the dough, and the warm scent of goodies baking in the oven makes everyone happy. I remember baking cookies and cakes with my mom as a child and am thankful for the cozy memories of licking batter bowls and beaters. I want my kids to have those same memories, even if it means a little sugar once in a while.

My girls know they only get dessert after eating a healthy dinner, and often that is a helpful motivator at dinnertime. Everyday desserts can even be healthy. Dessert can be a simple bowl of fresh strawberries after dinner, a fruit crisp baked with oats and nuts, like my Healthy Raspberry-Apple Crisp with Coconut-Oat Topping (page 212) or wholesome Berry Shortcake (page 218).

Making desserts from scratch is a good way to stay healthy. Store-bought cookies and other treats can contain unnecessary amounts of sugar, trans fats, and chemicals. My policy is to never buy store-bought desserts other than good-quality chocolate. If I want cookies, I make them myself, so that I know exactly what is in them. That habit also means there is less temptation around the house on a daily basis. If I'm going to eat a dessert, I want it to be really good. To me, eating a mediocre cookie is not worth the calories. I would much rather have just one square of really good chocolate or a serving of a fresh homemade dessert.

These sweet and tart bars are the perfect summer treat for packing in picnic baskets, taking to the beach, or nibbling with an afternoon cup of tea. I like to cut each bar into quarters, so that they are bite-size.

Apricot Almond Crumble Bars

2¼ cups all-purpose flour

½ cup sugar

1 teaspoon baking powder

¼ teaspoon salt

¾ cup virgin coconut oil or butter, at room temperature (not melted)

½ teaspoon almond extract

¼ cup sliced almonds, plus 1 tablespoon

4 to 5 apricots, halved and pitted

¼ cup apricot jam

Virgin coconut oil is prized for its numerous health benefits, including promoting weight loss and healthy skin and boosting immunity. Coconut oil can be used in place of other fats in cooking and baking. Many people even add a tablespoon of melted coconut oil to smoothies to obtain its health benefits.

Preheat the oven to 375°F. Spray an 8-inch square baking dish with cooking spray, then line it with parchment paper and spray again.

In a medium bowl, stir together the flour, sugar, baking powder, and salt. Mix in the coconut oil or butter, almond extract, and ¼ cup sliced almonds until combined and crumbly. Press half of the mixture into the bottom of the prepared baking dish. Lay the apricot halves, cut side down, on the flour mixture. In a small heatproof bowl, microwave the apricot jam for 10 seconds. With a pastry brush, brush a light coating of jam over the apricots. Crumble the remaining half of the flour mixture over and around the apricots.

Bake for 40 minutes until the crumble topping is golden brown. Sprinkle with the remaining 1 tablespoon of sliced almonds. Cool completely before cutting into bars.

Makes 9 (2½-inch) squares or 36 bite-size squares

My favorite version of this recipe contains coffee ice cream. The coffee ice cream and chocolate cookie crust are the perfect combination of flavors after dinner. Since most coffee ice creams are caffeinated, I choose vanilla or strawberry flavors for the kids. These mini ice cream pies would be a wonderful alternative to cupcakes at a birthday party.

Mini Ice Cream Pies

16 chocolate sandwich cookies (such as Oreo)

4 tablespoons butter, melted

2 pints good-quality ice cream, any flavor

1 cup chocolate chips

1 tablespoon butter

1 tablespoon corn syrup

¼ cup milk

½ cup toasted nuts, chopped (optional)

2 tablespoons sprinkles (optional)

Step away from the grocery-store cake! Choose easy desserts that can be made a day ahead of time instead. The taste is incomparable, and your guests will appreciate the homemade effort.

Preheat the oven to 350°F. Spray a muffin pan with cooking spray.

To make the crust cups, pulse the cookies in a food processor until finely ground. Add the butter to the ground cookies and pulse until combined. Press 2 tablespoons of cookie crumbs into the bottoms and up the sides of eight muffin cups. Bake for 15 minutes. Cool completely. Place the muffin pan with the cookie cups in the freezer for 15 minutes to make removing the cups easier. Remove from the freezer, turn the pan upside down, and tap the back until the cups fall out. If they stick, try heating the underside of the pan with hot water for 10 seconds.

Scoop ice cream into the crust cups. An ice-cream scoop makes this easy and creates a nicely shaped pie. Place the ice cream pies back in the muffin tin. Cover with plastic wrap and freeze, for up to three days, until ready to use.

To make the fudge sauce, set a heatproof bowl over a saucepan of shallow simmering water to create a double boiler. Pour the chocolate chips into the bowl and stir until melted. Stir in the butter, corn syrup, and milk until smooth and combined. Let fudge cool to room temperature.

The next step is pouring the fudge sauce over the ice cream. Because the fudge tends to run off the top of the ice cream, first spread a small, ½ teaspoon-size dollop of fudge on the very top of the ice cream domes and place the ice cream pies back into the freezer for 2 minutes until the chocolate dollops have hardened. Then pour the rest of the fudge on the tops of the pies. Top with nuts or sprinkles, if desired. Serve immediately, or return to the freezer until you're ready to serve.

Makes 8 cupcake-size pies

Broiling peaches makes them even sweeter and juicier. When peaches are ripe in the summer, I like to pair them with vanilla ice cream for an easy refreshing treat. One of my favorite traditional Italian adult desserts is almond biscotti dipped in Vin Santo dessert wine. This recipe combines those flavors with the peaches and ice cream. Omit the wine for kids. Serve the parfaits in wine glasses for adults and in clear plastic cups for kids for the perfect summer entertaining dessert.

Broiled Peach and Biscotti Parfaits

4 peaches
4 teaspoons granulated sugar
1 pint good-quality vanilla bean ice cream
8 large almond biscotti or cantucci
½ cup Vin Santo wine (for adults only)

Preheat the broiler with the rack in the top of the oven. Cut the peaches in half and remove the pits. Place them skin side down on a cookie sheet and sprinkle the cut sides with sugar. Broil for 3 minutes, until the sugar has browned. Remove from the oven.

Chop half the biscotti into ½-inch pieces. Reserve the other half for garnish. Place the chopped biscotti in the bottoms of four glasses or cups. Top each with a small scoop of ice cream. Place one peach half on top of the ice cream. Top the peach half with another small scoop of ice cream. Pour Vin Santo over the ice cream and top with the other peach half. Serve with the remaining biscotti as a garnish in the glass or cup or next to it on a plate.

Serves 4

Vin Santo is available at Whole Foods and other specialty stores.

LIFE TIP

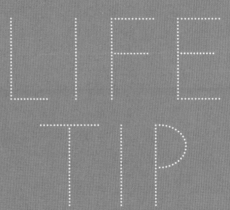

Wine-country vacations can be a lot of fun for kids too! Wine regions usually have lots of open spaces for kids to run around, bike rentals, and orchards to explore, and the atmosphere is usually quite casual and relaxed. One of my favorite family trips was to Sonoma, California, when our older daughter was just one year old. We spent the day pushing the jogging stroller from our hotel along the bike path through beautiful vineyards and into town. We all enjoyed stopping at the cheese and wine shops and tasting samples of artisan cheeses, crackers, and chocolates. After picking up a bag of our favorite selections, we enjoyed a casual picnic in the park, where our little one could practice her newfound walking skills.

Our family also loves to take day trips to Santa Ynez—Santa Barbara's own wine country—just a half an hour away. We go to Santa Ynez in the summer to pick blueberries and in the fall for apple picking and grape harvest barbecues. The girls like to stop at a horse farm or two and admire the cows out the window on our drive. The miles of vineyards and rolling hills always make me feel as though I've escaped to another country where life moves at a much slower pace.

Dried lavender flowers add a subtle floral note that transforms basic vanilla cupcakes into an easy elegant treat. This lemon glaze is the simplest icing there is and is perfectly tangy and sweet without any of the fat of traditional frostings. Lavender Cupcakes are the perfect dessert for baby showers and birthday parties.

Lavender Cupcakes

1¼ cups all-purpose flour

1 teaspoon baking powder

¼ teaspoon salt

1 level teaspoon dried culinary lavender

¾ cup granulated sugar

½ cup butter, at room temperature

2 large eggs, at room temperature

½ cup milk, at room temperature

½ teaspoon vanilla extract

1 cup confectioners' sugar

2½ to 3 tablespoons fresh lemon juice

12 fresh lavender flowers, for garnish (optional)

Preheat the oven to 350°F. Place paper liners in a muffin pan.

For the cupcakes, in a medium bowl whisk together the flour, baking powder, and salt. Set aside. In a food processor, blend the lavender and sugar until combined and the lavender is finely chopped. In the bowl of a mixer, cream together the butter and lavender sugar until light and creamy, beating for about 3 minutes at medium speed. Beat the eggs into the butter mixture one at a time. Stir in the milk and vanilla. Gently stir in the flour mixture until just combined. Spoon the batter into the muffin cups. Bake for 15 to 17 minutes, until a toothpick inserted in the middle of a cupcake comes out clean. Cool on a wire rack.

Make the glaze by whisking together, in a small bowl, the confectioners' sugar and lemon juice until smooth. Spoon the glaze over the cooled cupcakes. Garnish with fresh lavender flowers, if desired.

Makes 12 cupcakes

LIFE TIP

Even when we mommies are just staying home with the kids, it can brighten our mood to take two minutes and put on a coat of mascara and lip gloss. It boosts our confidence and makes us feel like the Yummy Mummies we are on the inside. For even more glamour, try red lipstick. My favorite classic red lipstick is "Lover" by Chanel.

Pomegranate Chocolate Chunk Sherbet

2½ cups pomegranate juice
1 cup whole milk
¼ cup heavy cream
¼ cup sugar
1 ounce dark chocolate, chopped

Whisk the pomegranate juice, milk, cream, and sugar
together and pour into an ice cream maker. Freeze
according to the manufacturer's instructions. Stir in
chocolate chunks and transfer to a freezer-safe container. Freeze for 2 hours or eat immediately.

Makes about 1 pint

Just one square.
Tai Tai and my
mom always keep
a bar of good-
quality chocolate
on hand. Their
theory is that one
square of choco-
late per night
won't hurt and
is a good way to
stay healthy while
not depriving
oneself of sweet
treats.

My aunt Ginny and Grandma Tai Tai once brought me a bag of cookies from the Brown Butter Cookie Company in Cayucos, California, raving about how wonderful and famous they are in central California. After one bite I knew why they were so revered and set out to make my own brown butter sea salt cookies. I think this recipe comes very close to the original. This is my favorite cookie recipe, and it has been wildly popular with my friends and family. I know you'll love it too.

Salted Brown Butter Cookies

¾ cup (1½ sticks) unsalted butter
½ cup lightly packed brown sugar
1 teaspoon vanilla extract
1⅓ cups all-purpose flour
1 teaspoon baking powder
Coarse-flake sea salt for sprinkling (preferably fleur de sel)

Preheat the oven to 325°F. Line a cookie sheet with parchment paper.

In a saucepan over medium heat, melt the butter until it starts to brown. When the butter has browned and is ready, the foam will have subsided and it will have turned a nutty color. Watch closely so as not to burn the butter. Pour the browned butter into a medium bowl and stir in the brown sugar and vanilla. In a small bowl, whisk the flour and baking powder together. With a spoon, stir the flour mixture into the butter mixture until combined. Drop the dough by tablespoonfuls onto the cookie sheet. Sprinkle with sea salt and lightly press it into the top of cookies. Bake for 12 minutes.

Makes 13 cookies

LIFE TIP

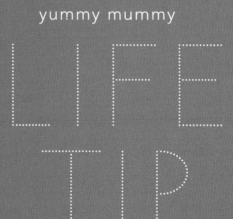

Never show up empty-handed. Try to always bring a small gift for the host or hostess of any get-together. My mom has a small cabinet that's always filled with possible hostess gifts. Great gift ideas include candles, fresh fruit, a bottle of wine, a good olive oil or vinegar, tea, or cookies.

For over a hundred years, shortbread has been a favorite treat with the Yummy Mummies in my family. Shortbread also happens to be one of the simplest cookies to make and requires just a few ingredients. This recipe includes two of my favorite flavors together: chocolate and hazelnut.

Chocolate Hazelnut Shortbread

½ cup butter, at room temperature
1¼ cups all-purpose flour
½ cup chocolate hazelnut spread, such as Nutella
1 ounce dark chocolate, chopped (about ¼ cup)
1 teaspoon fleur de sel or other good-quality coarse sea salt

In a medium bowl, mix all the ingredients together with your hands. Shape into a 2-inch-wide log on a large piece of plastic wrap. Tightly wrap and refrigerate overnight or at least 2 hours.

Preheat the oven to 350°F, and line a cookie sheet with parchment paper. Using a sharp knife, cut the log into ¼-inch slices. Place the slices on the cookie sheet and bake for 8 to 10 minutes. The cookies should be just set, not crisp. Cool on a wire rack.

Makes about 15 cookies

My grandmother on my father's side of the family always made these pinwheel cookies. They are quite possibly the tastiest and most addictive cookies I've ever eaten. They are like a brownie wrapped in a brown-sugar cookie. These cookies are not the healthiest, but they are so good that they must be bookmarked for a special occasion. I make these every year at Christmastime to share with friends and family, and when I do so, I always think of my grandma.

Fudgy Pinwheel Cookies

1 cup all-purpose flour

½ teaspoon salt

¼ teaspoon baking powder

½ cup packed brown sugar

¼ cup unsalted butter, plus 1 tablespoon, at room temperature

1 large egg yolk

½ teaspoon vanilla extract

1 to 2 tablespoons water

1 cup bittersweet chocolate chips

½ cup sweetened condensed milk

1 cup chopped walnuts or pecans

To make the dough, whisk the flour, salt, and baking powder together in a medium bowl. In the bowl of a mixer, cream the brown sugar and ¼ cup butter for 2 minutes. Add the egg yolk and vanilla and beat until combined. Add the flour mixture and beat until combined. Add water 1 tablespoon at a time until the dough comes together. Transfer the dough to a large sheet of waxed paper and roll out into a 12 × 9-inch rectangle.

To make the chocolate layer, in a medium glass bowl melt the chocolate chips and the 1 tablespoon butter in the microwave at 20-second intervals, stirring in between, until chocolate is almost completely smooth and melted, taking care not to burn the chocolate. Stir in the condensed milk and nuts until combined.

Press the chocolate mixture over the dough on the waxed paper, leaving a 1-inch edge on the long sides. Using the waxed paper to help, start at one long edge and roll the dough into a log. Wrap in the waxed paper and twist the ends. Chill in refrigerator for at least 2 hours and up to two days. Alternately, freeze for up to two weeks.

Preheat the oven to 375°F, and line a cookie sheet with parchment paper. Cut the dough into ½-inch slices and place 1 inch apart on the cookie sheet. Bake for 10 minutes. Cool slightly. These cookies are best enjoyed warm, but will keep for several days in an airtight container.

Makes about 25 cookies

LIFE TIP

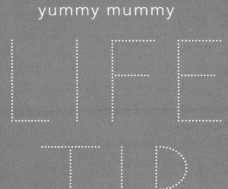

Write down your family's favorite recipes to hand down to your kids and their kids after them. Family recipes are an intimate way of connecting generations. Looking through your parents' and grandparents' old cookbooks is also fun. Tai Tai loaned me her mother's old cocktail cookbook, *Here's How: Mixed Drinks*, which was published in 1941. The cover is hand-painted wood with brass hinges and the pages have yellowed with age. Looking at the worn "Christmas Eggnog" page, I imagine my grandmother and her mother sipping the festive drink at glamorous holiday parties in the 1940s and 1950s.

Healthy Raspberry-Apple Crisp with Coconut-Oat Topping

5 cups sliced apples (about 6 apples)

2 teaspoons cinnamon

½ teaspoon nutmeg

1 tablespoon lemon juice

⅓ cup agave syrup

1 cup raspberries

1 cup oats

½ cup natural flaked or shredded coconut

½ cup lightly packed brown sugar

¼ cup all-purpose flour

⅓ cup coconut oil or butter, melted

Most apple pie and crisp recipes call for peeled apples. I always leave the skins on to retain the maximum amount of vitamins—and save time. Plus, that's the way my mom always did it.

Preheat the oven to 375°F. Coat a 9-inch pie dish, 8-inch square baking dish, or six 4-inch mini pie dishes lightly with cooking spray.

For the filling, in a large bowl toss the apples with 1 teaspoon cinnamon, nutmeg, lemon juice, and agave to coat. Gently fold in the raspberries. Spoon the mixture into the baking dish.

For the topping, stir together the oats, coconut, brown sugar, flour, and the remaining teaspoon of cinnamon in a medium bowl. Stir in the coconut oil or melted butter to combine. Sprinkle the oat mixture over the apples and bake for 40 minutes or until the apples are tender.

Serves 6

Store-bought ladyfinger cookies are a delicious shortcut for desserts. Strawberry Lemonade Tiramisu is a cool variation on the traditional coffee tiramisu. This recipe is best made one day in advance.

Strawberry Lemonade Tiramisu

1 cup whipping cream, cold

8 ounces mascarpone cheese, at room temperature

⅓ cup lemon curd

1 cup lemonade

1 (6-ounce) box ladyfinger cookies

2 cups fresh strawberries, stems removed and sliced

½ cup strawberries, for garnish

Lemon slices or peel, for garnish

Fresh mint, for garnish

For an adults-only version, add 1 ounce of limoncello liquor to the lemonade.

In the bowl of a mixer fitted with a whisk attachment, beat the cream until stiff enough to hold soft peaks. Add the mascarpone and lemon curd and continue to beat until just combined.

Pour the lemonade into a large shallow bowl. Quickly dip the ladyfingers in the lemonade and place the soaked cookies into an 8-inch square baking dish or six 4-inch individual bowls. Ladyfingers can be cut to fit the dish. Spread ½ inch of the mascarpone cream over the ladyfingers. Arrange a single layer of strawberry slices over the cream. Continue layering soaked ladyfingers, cream, and strawberries. The number of layers will vary depending on the size of the dish. Garnish with strawberries, lemon slices or peel, and mint, if desired.

Serves 6

Val, my great-grandmother, was asked to be the head dietician at the American Club in Shanghai because of her reputation as a fabulous cook with a flair for entertaining. Val taught the cooks to make her lemon pie and soon patrons were asking for it daily. The recipe was passed down to my grandmother, Tai Tai, and became my mother's favorite dessert when she was growing up. My mom would ask for this lemon pie whenever she came home from college or craved a sweet bite of comfort. This pie has a unique meringue shell, making it lighter than most lemon pies with pastry crusts.

Grandma's Lemon Angel Pie

3 large eggs whites

¼ teaspoon cream of tartar

1¾ cups sugar

2 tablespoons cornstarch

¼ teaspoon salt

3 large egg yolks

6 tablespoons lemon juice

¾ cup water

1½ teaspoons lemon zest, plus more for garnish

1½ cups whipping cream

To make the shell, preheat the oven to 275°F. Beat the egg whites until stiff. Add the cream of tartar and 1 cup sugar. Beat until stiff and glossy. Pour into a 9-inch pie dish and spread the mixture up the sides of the dish. Bake for 20 minutes. Increase the temperature to 300°F and bake for 30 minutes more. Cool.

To make the lemon filling, in a medium bowl mix ¾ cup sugar with cornstarch and salt. In small bowl, stir the 3 egg yolks with 1 tablespoon lemon juice. Stir the egg mixture into the sugar mixture. In a small saucepan, bring ¾ cup water to a simmer. Add the egg mixture, the remaining 5 tablespoons lemon juice, and the lemon zest. Stir constantly until thickened, about 5 minutes. Cool completely.

In the bowl of a mixer fitted with a whisk attachment, whip the cream. Spread half of whipped cream over the meringue shell. Pour all of the lemon custard over the cream. Top with the rest of the cream. Garnish with lemon zest.

Serves 6

This wholesome dessert is made up of an oat cake topped with freshly whipped cream and piles of berries. This berry shortcake is a rustic, easy, and deconstructed version of traditional strawberry shortcake, and I like it even better. The fresh berries and cream are the stars of this dessert, so be sure to get them in every bite and serve in the summer when ripe berries are at their peak. This dessert works just as well for an afternoon snack with tea or brunch as it does for dessert.

Berry Shortcake

1 cup strawberries, chopped

Juice of ½ lemon

¼ cup sugar, plus 1 tablespoon

1½ cups all-purpose flour

1 cup rolled oats

1 tablespoon baking powder

¼ teaspoon salt

1 large egg, lightly beaten

½ cup unsalted butter, melted

½ cup milk

1½ cups whipping cream

2 tablespoons confectioners' sugar

1 teaspoon vanilla extract

4 cups fresh berries

Fresh mint leaves, for garnish

Preheat the oven to 425°F. Line a baking sheet with parchment paper.

Place the chopped strawberries, lemon juice, and 1 tablespoon of sugar in a small bowl. Set it aside to macerate.

For the shortcake, whisk together the flour, oats, ¼ cup sugar, baking powder, and salt in a medium bowl. In another medium bowl, stir together the egg, melted butter, and milk. Stir the egg, butter, and milk mixture into the dry ingredients until just combined. Place the dough on the parchment-lined baking sheet and spread into a 9-inch disk with floured hands. Bake for 12 minutes. Remove from the oven and cool slightly. Poke holes over the top of cake with a toothpick.

Transfer the chopped strawberries to a food processor and puree. Spread the strawberry sauce over the top of cake. In the bowl of a mixer, beat the cream, confectioners' sugar, and vanilla on high speed with the whisk attachment until stiff peaks form. Spread the whipped cream over the strawberry sauce. Top with fresh berries and garnish with mint leaves.

Serves 6

Cooking bananas in brown sugar and butter creates a crisp crust that takes bananas to another level. Serve these crepe pockets on plates or eat with hands. I can't wait to make these with my girls at their sleepover parties when they are older!

Caramelized Banana Split Crepes

1 cup milk

2 large eggs

1 tablespoon sugar

1 teaspoon vanilla extract

5 tablespoons melted butter

1 cup all-purpose flour

2 bananas

3 tablespoons brown sugar

1 pint vanilla ice cream

1 cup fresh strawberries, sliced

2 tablespoons chocolate sauce (store-bought, or see
    page 190 for an easy homemade recipe)

Mint leaves, for garnish

For the crepes, in a medium bowl whisk the milk, eggs, sugar, vanilla, and 2 tablespoons of the melted butter until just combined. Whisk the flour into the wet ingredients. Lightly coat a 10-inch nonstick frying pan with cooking spray, butter, or oil and place it over medium heat. Pour about ⅓ cup of batter into the frying pan and immediately swirl the pan, so that the batter covers the surface in one thin layer. Cook for about 1 to 2 minutes until the bottom has set and is starting to brown. Flip the crepe and continue to cook another minute. Remove from the pan, and continue making crepes until all batter has been used up. You will have about 8 crepes. Let crepes cool.

For the caramelized bananas, peel the bananas and cut them in half length-wise and then again crosswise, so that each is cut into four pieces. Heat the remaining 3 tablespoons of butter in a frying pan over high heat. Stir in the brown sugar. Add the bananas and gently turn to coat. Cook 2 minutes per side. Remove the bananas from the pan and cool slightly.

Fold crepes in half, and then in half again so that they form triangles. Open one fold and place bananas and strawberries inside each of the 4 pockets. Add one small scoop of ice cream and drizzle with chocolate sauce. Garnish with mint. Wrap the remaining crepes with plastic wrap and save for another day.

Serves 4

In the 1940s Tai Tai was a young British citizen living in Hong Kong, a British colony. She was nineteen years old when the Japanese invaded and forced her into an internment camp. She was a prisoner of war for three years, and it was in the camp that she fell in love with another prisoner—a Scottish banker. Though they had to keep their romance secret while they were interned, Tai Tai and Bill married just hours after being released from camp. It was only natural that Tai Tai had a Scottish dessert recipe in her repertoire to wow her man. Light, beautiful, and delicious, Tai Tai's Raspberry Soufflé did the trick. Although Tai Tai's recipe was served chilled, I prefer these mousselike soufflés frozen. Freezing also means this recipe does not need the gelatin or egg yolk called for to stabilize the original recipe.

Frozen Scottish Raspberry Soufflé

Tai Tai's original recipe called for raw eggs. To avoid salmonella concerns I use dried egg whites, which are pasteurized. Dried egg white powder is available in the baking aisle of many grocery and natural foods stores, including Whole Foods.

1½ cups raspberries, plus more for garnish

1 tablespoon lemon juice

2 tablespoons pasteurized dried egg whites

⅓ cup granulated sugar

⅔ cup cold heavy whipping cream, plus more for garnish

2 tablespoons confectioners' sugar, plus more for garnish

Puree the raspberries with the lemon juice in a food processor or blender. Press the puree through a mesh sieve into a small bowl and discard the seeds.

In a large bowl, whip the dried egg whites with 6 tablespoons of warm water until almost stiff. Slowly add the granulated sugar and continue to beat until stiff peaks form.

In another large bowl, whip the cream with the confectioners' sugar until soft peaks form.

Fold the whipped cream and raspberry puree into the egg whites until combined, taking care not to break the whipped egg whites.

Use 2-inch strips of parchment paper to make a collar around the top edge of four 6-ounce ramekins. Tape the ends of the parchment paper together. Pour the raspberry mixture into the prepared ramekins.

Freeze for 1 hour, or up to one day in advance. After 1 hour, remove the parchment paper collars, cover with plastic wrap, and return to the freezer if serving later. Let the soufflés thaw at room temperature for 10 minutes before serving.

Garnish with raspberries, whipped cream, and confectioners' sugar.

Serves 4

One of my dear mommy friends and her family put on a swanky pre-Thanksgiving, or Friends-giving, dinner the week before Thanksgiving every year. It's a wonderful time for us to get together, without the kids, and celebrate our friendships and good food. My friend Sarah always makes a few turkeys and hams (yes, *a few*—there are over a hundred people at this party) and the guests bring side dishes and desserts. I always volunteer to bring dessert, since it's not every day I indulge in pie, trifle, or cake making. This trifle is my favorite Thanksgiving recipe yet, and judging by the empty dish after the party and kind comments from readers on my blog, it's a crowd-pleaser that's sure to become a tradition in your family too.

Pumpkin and Chocolate Mousse Trifle

When you're asked to make a dessert for a special occasion, try one that can be made a day in advance and you'll keep party time stress-free.

5 large egg yolks

¼ cup water

⅓ cup confectioners' sugar, plus 2 tablespoons

3 cups cold whipping cream

8 ounces good-quality bittersweet chocolate (60 to 70 percent cacao), chopped

1¼ cups canned pumpkin

1½ teaspoons pumpkin pie spice

2 tablespoons brown sugar

2 (10-ounce) frozen pound cakes, thawed, and cut into ¾-inch slices

2 tablespoons bourbon (optional, adults only)

Fresh raspberries, sugared cranberries (page 18), pumpkin seeds, or shaved chocolate, for garnish

Set the bowl of an electric mixer over a saucepan of shallow simmering water. Add the egg yolks, water, and ⅓ cup confectioners' sugar and whisk constantly until the mixture is frothy, beginning to thicken, and has reached 150°F. Remove from the heat and beat with an electric mixer for 3 minutes, until thickened. In another small bowl over the simmering water, melt the chocolate. Remove from the heat and let cool slightly. Divide the egg mixture into two medium bowls. Stir the cooled chocolate into one bowl. Into the other bowl stir the pumpkin, pumpkin pie spice, and brown sugar. In another bowl, beat the whipping cream and 2 tablespoons confectioners' sugar at high speed until stiff peaks form. Fold 1½ cups whipped cream into the chocolate mixture, and 1½ cups into the pumpkin mixture.

Place a layer of pound cake in the bottom of a trifle dish, large bowl, or individual dishes. Brush with a little bourbon. Spoon a 1-inch layer of pumpkin mousse over the cake. Top with a second layer of cake. Brush with bourbon. Spoon a 1-inch layer of chocolate mousse over this layer of cake. Top with a third layer of cake and again brush with bourbon. Top with the remaining whipped cream and garnish with raspberries or chocolate. Chill overnight.

Serves 6 to 8

breakfast and brunch

Apple Oat Muffins

Apple-Cinnamon Puff Pancake

Blueberry Oat Scones

California Egg Sandwiches

Low-Fat Pear and Cinnamon Chip Coffee Cake

Tropical Granola

Eggs Baked in Phyllo Cups

Whole Wheat Banana Walnut Bread

Overnight Berry French Toast

Peanut Butter and Jelly Granola Bars

Cherry Almond Muffins

Potato and Artichoke Frittata

Swiss Chard Strata

Strawberry Rhubarb Baked Oatmeal

Kefir Berry Power Smoothie

Chocolate Almond Smoothie

GOOD MORNING, SUNSHINE!

With hectic school and work schedules, lazy weekend mornings can be a great time to spend with family over a relaxing meal. Phil used to pick up bagel egg sandwiches or buttery scones early on weekend mornings. He would arrive home to the three of us girls still in pajamas, me sipping coffee and the girls watching cartoons. I couldn't be bothered cooking. After all, it was the weekend and I deserved a break from the long week of endless cooking and dishes. Weren't nightly dinners, lunchbox preparations, and snack fetching enough?

One Saturday morning as Phil was about to leave for our favorite bakery for muffins and scones, I stopped him. I was planning on going on a run later and didn't want to feel as though I had just eaten something without any nutrition. I decided to make a healthier batch of scones. I replaced some of the flour with heart-healthy oats, cut down on the sugar, and added fresh organic berries. To our surprise we liked the healthy homemade scones even better than those from our favorite bakery. They were on the table in less time than it took to go buy them and were much less expensive.

The girls and I now plan on cooking a healthy breakfast together on most weekend mornings. We sit down together to plan our day in the kitchen breakfast nook as the sun washes through the window. The mood at brunch is more relaxed than at dinnertime, when the kids (and mommy) can be overtired and feel rushed to get on to bathing and bedtime. Dinnertime is important, but sometimes both parents cannot be there for dinner. When daddy is a physician who works unpredictable hours, it often can mean that dinner is just us girls. I know that may be the reality for you too. A weekend brunch together can make up for a lost dinnertime or two during the week and starts the day on a good note.

Kids feel more confident when they have a good understanding of the events of the day or week ahead. Sitting down for breakfast is a great time for parents to give kids a quick rundown of their schedules, but it's also important for their physical and mental health. Breakfast is considered by many to be the most important meal of the day. Unfortunately, many kids are sent to school either without breakfast or having eaten cereal containing more sugar than a couple of cookies. Moms and dads often have the same problem. We find ourselves so busy packing lunches and getting everyone dressed and out the door that we forget or don't have time to eat breakfast. We get to work feeling tired and thinking we need another cup of coffee when what we really need is fuel in the form of real food. Then ten or eleven o'clock rolls around and we are ravenous. The easiest thing to eat seems like the best option. Cookies? Why not?

The way we eat at the start of the day sets the tone for the rest of the day. Quick healthy breakfasts always need to be available. Keeping a container of homemade granola (see Tropical Granola, page 244) around to sprinkle over a bowl of yogurt with fresh berries is a way to have an easy, healthy breakfast for kids and parents. California Egg Sandwiches (page 240) are much leaner and less processed than fast-food egg sandwiches, but every bit as delicious and fast and even pack in a serving of greens. You can send kids to school knowing their bodies and brains have the proper nutrition to thrive.

When I was a schoolteacher, kids would routinely arrive without having had an adequate breakfast. They were easy to spot. Some kids would have a hard time concentrating in the mornings, because they had had only sugary cereals, sweets, and, yes, even soda. Others hadn't eaten anything at all and would complain of being hungry long before recess. Both of these avoidable situations were detrimental to those students' ability to learn (and their classmates'). It's not the kids' job to make smart breakfast choices. It's our job as parents to make healthy foods available and appealing.

Whether it's a quick weekday breakfast or a leisurely weekend brunch, the old adage that the first meal of the day is the most important seems to hold true. Try making some of these simple recipes for your family. See what happens when you sit down together on weekend mornings and share a special homemade brunch. Pay attention to how much better you feel and how much better your kids behave when they have had a healthy breakfast. Brunch is the perfect time to share a relaxed meal with your family, connect, and plan the day.

This recipe is the ultimate health muffin. Oats add nutrition, and applesauce adds fat-free moisture. These muffins are best served warm from the oven.

Apple Oat Muffins

1 tablespoon butter

1 small apple, halved, cored, and thinly sliced

½ teaspoon cinnamon

1 cup oats

1½ cups all-purpose flour

⅓ cup lightly packed brown sugar, plus 1 teaspoon

1½ teaspoons pumpkin pie spice (or a mixture of cinnamon and nutmeg)

½ teaspoon salt

1 tablespoon baking powder

2 large eggs, lightly beaten

1 cup milk

⅓ cup applesauce

1 tablespoon coconut oil, melted

1 teaspoon vanilla extract

1 small apple, halved, cored, and diced

Preheat the oven to 375°F. Place paper liners in a muffin pan.

Heat 1 tablespoon butter in a skillet over medium heat. Add the sliced apples and ½ teaspoon cinnamon and sauté until just softened, about 4 minutes. Remove from the heat and set aside.

In a medium bowl, whisk together the oats, flour, brown sugar, pumpkin pie spice, salt, and baking powder. In another medium bowl, stir together the eggs, milk, applesauce, oil, and vanilla. Gently stir the wet ingredients into the dry ingredients. Fold in the diced apples.

Spoon the batter into the muffin cups. Place 2 to 3 apple slices on the top of each muffin. Sprinkle the apple slices with the remaining teaspoon of brown sugar. Bake for 15 minutes or until an inserted toothpick comes out clean. Serve warm.

Makes 12 muffins

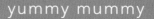

LIFE TIP

Before having kids I hated exercising. I forced myself to go to the gym, but was unhappy the entire time I was there. Once my first baby was born, I was happy to have an easy excuse to skip the gym—I had an infant who needed me around the clock. To my surprise, I quickly realized I missed exercise. I felt tired and grumpy without regular exercise and wanted to lose the forty pounds I had gained during my pregnancy. Once my daughter was old enough to stay in the gym childcare, I looked at the fitness class schedule and wrote down specific times on my calendar, so that I wouldn't forget or push my workouts aside. My mind felt clearer and my body felt healthier once I was back to a regular exercise routine. But something about exercise had shifted for me from my pre-baby days. I didn't hate the gym anymore—I really enjoyed it.

The one hour I spend at the gym a few days a week is the only time that is purely for me. That one hour when I can put on my headphones and be alone with my thoughts is crucial to my emotional well-being. I notice I'm a much nicer mommy on workout days. If you're like me and have a hard time getting motivated to exercise, try writing it on your calendar, so that it's a scheduled appointment in your day.

ARM FRESH EGGS $4.00
ANGE FREE - ORGANIC - FERTILE
Apples $2.00 - UP
GALAS
HOBART
CAPACITY 30 LBS. x 1 OZ.

German puff pancake is one recipe I vividly remember being excited about as a child. Not only was it deliciously sweet with some crisp edges and a soft center; it was just plain fun to make. There was something special about the way the edges puffed up along the sides of the pan. Mom always made it plain and served it with powdered sugar and a drizzle of fresh tart lemon juice over the top. In this recipe I've added apples and the warm flavors of cinnamon, nutmeg, and maple.

Apple-Cinnamon Puff Pancake

3 tablespoons butter

1 large apple, halved, cored, and thinly sliced

1 tablespoon brown sugar

1 teaspoon cinnamon

½ teaspoon nutmeg

3 large eggs

¾ cup milk

¾ cup all-purpose flour

2 tablespoons confectioners' sugar

Preheat the oven to 375°F.

Melt the butter in a 9-inch ovenproof skillet over medium heat. Add the apples. Sprinkle with brown sugar, cinnamon, and nutmeg. Stir to coat and cook for 2 minutes.

In a bowl, whisk the eggs, milk, and flour together. Pour over the apples. Bake for 15 to 20 minutes, until golden. Cut into 6 wedges. Sprinkle with confectioners' sugar and serve with maple syrup.

Serves 4 to 6

This healthier version of our favorite bakery breakfast treat is quick and easy to prepare. It is my go-to weekend-morning recipe that the girls and I make over and over.

Blueberry Oat Scones

1½ cups all-purpose flour

1½ cups rolled oats

1 teaspoon lemon zest

¼ cup plus ½ tablespoon turbinado sugar

1 tablespoon baking powder

¼ teaspoon salt

½ cup cold unsalted butter, cut into small cubes

1 large egg, lightly beaten

½ cup low-fat buttermilk

1 cup fresh blueberries

Preheat the oven to 425°F. Line a cookie sheet with parchment paper.

In the bowl of a mixer, stir the flour, oats, lemon zest, ¼ cup sugar, baking powder, and salt to combine. Add the butter and mix on medium for 2 minutes. Add the egg and continue beating until combined. Slowly add the buttermilk and beat until just moistened. Gently fold in the blueberries. Scoop heaping ¼-cup balls of dough and place on the prepared cookie sheet 2 inches apart. Sprinkle the top of the scones with the remaining ½ tablespoon of sugar. Bake until golden brown, 12 to 14 minutes. Cool on a wire rack.

Makes 9 to 10 scones

LIFE TIP

Homemade gifts are inexpensive and personal. Scone mix makes a sweet gift for teachers, family, and friends. Combine the dry ingredients and place in a 1-quart canning jar. Place dried fruit such as cranberries or cherries in a sandwich bag on top of the dry ingredients. Attach an ingredient list and recipe, so the recipient can quickly make the scones at home.

add:
1/2 cup unsalted butter, melted
1/3 cup milk
1 egg, lightly beaten

Stir top 3 ingredients together. Add
dry ingredients and stir until just
moistened. Scoop 1/2 cup balls of
dough and place on cookie sheet a
few inches apart. Bake until light
brown, about 15 minutes. Cool
slightly on rack.

CHERRY
OAT
SCONE MIX

Healthy egg sandwiches are a satisfying way to eat veggies and protein early in the day. These sandwiches are a great alternative to fatty fast-food egg sandwiches and easy to take on the go.

California Egg Sandwiches

2 English muffins
2 thin slices sharp cheddar cheese
1 tablespoon butter
2 large eggs
½ cup arugula or baby spinach
½ avocado, peeled, pitted, and sliced

Lightly toast the English muffins. Immediately lay one slice of cheese on each of the cut sides of the top halves of the toasted muffins, so that the cheese melts.

Melt the butter in a medium skillet over medium heat. Add eggs to the pan and cook to desired doneness. I like to use egg rings to make perfectly round fried eggs, but they are not necessary.

Place arugula on bottom halves of the English muffins. Top each with a fried egg and 2 or 3 slices of avocado. Sprinkle with salt and pepper. Place the muffin tops on the bottoms.

Makes 2 sandwiches

Low-Fat Pear and Cinnamon Chip Coffee Cake

1¾ cups all-purpose flour
1 cup sugar
2¼ teaspoons baking powder
½ teaspoon salt
1 teaspoon cinnamon
1 large egg
½ cup milk
¼ cup pear sauce or applesauce
1 tablespoon vegetable oil
½ cup cinnamon chips
2 small pears, halved, cored, and sliced
2 tablespoons butter, melted

Preheat the oven to 400°F. Coat a square or round 8-inch baking pan with cooking spray.

For the cake, whisk together 1½ cups flour, ½ cup sugar, baking powder, salt, and ½ teaspoon cinnamon. Stir together the egg, milk, pear sauce, and oil. Slowly stir the dry ingredients into the wet ingredients. Fold in the cinnamon chips. Pour into the prepared pan. Arrange the pears over the top.

For the streusel topping, in a small bowl stir together the remaining ½ cup sugar, ¼ cup flour, and ½ teaspoon cinnamon. Stir in the butter, and sprinkle the mixture over the top of the pears and batter.

Bake for 25 to 30 minutes or until a toothpick inserted in the center comes out clean.

Serves 6

The kids and I love to make a batch of granola to eat for breakfast and snack on throughout the week. Homemade granola is healthier and fresher tasting than most store-bought granola. It's a fun recipe for kids to help with, as they love to use their hands to mix the ingredients together in a big bowl. Our granola is different every time we make it, but these tropical ingredients are our favorites. Try substituting your favorite nuts and fruits to create your own signature granola.

Tropical Granola

3 cups rolled oats

¾ cup macadamia nuts

¼ cup walnut pieces

½ cup unsweetened flaked coconut

2 tablespoons flaxseeds

¼ cup lightly packed brown sugar

½ teaspoon salt

¼ cup honey

2½ tablespoons coconut oil

1 cup dried tropical fruits, such as pineapple, mango, and papaya

Preheat the oven to 300°F. Lightly coat a rimmed cookie sheet with cooking spray.

In a large bowl, stir together the oats, nuts, coconut, flaxseeds, brown sugar, and salt. Stir in the honey and coconut oil and combine. Spread the oat mixture on the cookie sheet in an even layer. Bake for 35 minutes, or until golden brown, stirring halfway through. Let cool completely on the cookie sheet.

Gently stir the dried fruit into the granola. Store in an airtight container.

Makes 6 servings

Storing your most frequently used baking ingredients and dry foods, like flours and cereals, on the counter in glass containers looks cute and frees up pantry space. My favorite storage containers can be found at Sur la Table and Cost Plus World Market.

Eggs Baked in Phyllo Cups

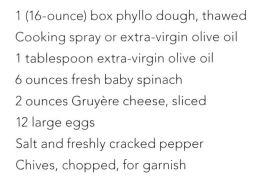

1 (16-ounce) box phyllo dough, thawed
Cooking spray or extra-virgin olive oil
1 tablespoon extra-virgin olive oil
6 ounces fresh baby spinach
2 ounces Gruyère cheese, sliced
12 large eggs
Salt and freshly cracked pepper
Chives, chopped, for garnish

Preheat the oven to 400°F. Lightly coat a muffin pan with cooking spray.

Lay 5 sheets of phyllo dough on top of each other, spraying each sheet lightly with cooking spray or brushing with olive oil. Using a 4-inch round cookie cutter or a similar-size can or bowl to cut around, cut out 12 circles of dough. Press the circles into the muffin pan.

Heat 1 tablespoon olive oil in a large pan over medium heat. Add the spinach and a pinch of salt and pepper and toss until wilted. Distribute the wilted spinach among phyllo cups. Top each with a slice of cheese. Crack one egg into each cup. Bake until the eggs are cooked, but the yolks are still slightly runny, about 10 minutes. Season to taste with salt and pepper and garnish with chives.

Makes 12 egg cups

This recipe can be made in advance. Assemble up to 2 hours early, cover with plastic wrap, refrigerate, and then remove, unwrap, and bake when you're ready to eat.

This wholesome banana bread is a nutritional powerhouse—it is packed with ingredients like flaxseeds and walnuts and free of refined sugar.

Whole Wheat Banana Walnut Bread

1 cup raw turbinado sugar

½ cup butter, at room temperature

3 ripe bananas, mashed

2 large eggs, beaten

¾ cup all-purpose flour

½ cup whole-wheat flour

½ teaspoon salt

1 teaspoon baking soda

2 tablespoons flaxseeds

2 cups walnut halves

1 ounce dark chocolate, chopped (optional)

Butter can quickly be brought to room temperature in the microwave. Heat sticks of butter on a dish at 10-second intervals until softened.

Preheat the oven to 350°F. Coat a loaf pan with cooking spray, or butter, and flour.

In the bowl of a mixer, beat together the sugar and butter. Add the bananas and eggs and continue to beat until combined. In another medium bowl, whisk together the all-purpose flour, whole-wheat flour, salt, baking soda, and flaxseeds. Slowly mix the flour mixture into the wet ingredients until just combined, taking care not to overmix. With a spatula, stir in the walnuts. Mix in the chocolate pieces, if using. Pour the batter into the loaf pan.

Bake for 50 to 60 minutes, or until an inserted toothpick comes out clean. Check after 30 minutes and cover with foil if the top is getting too brown. Serve with cream cheese, if desired.

Makes 1 loaf

I love waking up on a leisurely weekend morning and popping a preassembled dish into the oven. I'm then able to watch cartoons with my girls while I sip my coffee instead of working in the kitchen. When you'd like to have a dish ready to go for a weekend morning, try this delicious baked French toast.

Overnight Berry French Toast

6 large eggs

2 cups milk

1 tablespoon maple syrup

Zest and juice of 1 small orange

1 teaspoon vanilla extract

1 baguette, cut into ½-inch diagonal slices

2 cups berries (any combination of raspberries, blackberries, or blueberries)

1½ tablespoons butter, melted

1 cup chopped walnuts

¼ cup lightly packed brown sugar

Coat a 9 × 13-inch baking dish with cooking spray. In a large bowl, whisk the eggs, milk, syrup, orange zest and juice, and vanilla together. Dip the bread slices in the egg mixture and arrange in two rows in the baking dish. Tuck berries between slices and along the edges. Pour remaining egg mixture over top of the bread and berries. Cover with plastic wrap and refrigerate overnight.

Remove the French toast from refrigerator and remove the plastic wrap. Preheat the oven to 375°F. In a small bowl, stir together the melted butter, walnuts, and brown sugar. Sprinkle over the bread and berries. Bake uncovered for 40 minutes. Check after 30 minutes and cover with foil if the top is getting too brown. Serve with maple syrup.

Serves 8

The last time I made these granola bars for a play date there was nothing but crumbs left in a matter of minutes. Packed with protein and fiber, these all-natural granola bars are perfect for breakfasts on the go, lunchboxes, after-school snacks, and soccer games. This is a great recipe for kids to help make, as they can pour all the ingredients in the bowl, stir, and pour the mixture themselves.

Peanut Butter and Jelly Granola Bars

2 cups rolled oats
⅓ cup all-purpose flour
2 tablespoons flaxseeds
½ cup lightly packed brown sugar
½ cup butter, melted
¾ cup peanut butter
⅓ cup raspberry jam

Preheat the oven to 350°F. Place a 12-inch square of parchment paper over an 8-inch square baking dish and press it down onto the bottom and up the sides of the dish.

In a large bowl, stir together the oats, flour, flaxseeds, and brown sugar. Stir in the melted butter and peanut butter. Press the oat mixture into the prepared baking dish, reserving ½ cup for topping. Spoon 4 lines of jam across the top of the oat mixture. Sprinkle the remaining ½ cup of oat mixture over the jam.

Bake for 20 minutes, or until slightly browned and firm. Cool completely, at least 1 hour. Cut into squares.

Makes about 9 bars

Almond flour produces a dense, hearty muffin with a subtle nutty flavor that I love with fresh cherries. It also adds fiber and protein.

Cherry Almond Muffins

1 cup all-purpose flour

1 cup almond flour

1 tablespoon baking powder

¼ teaspoon salt

½ cup sugar

1 large egg

1 cup milk

1 teaspoon vanilla extract

¼ cup coconut oil or butter, melted

¾ cup cherries, pitted and roughly chopped

1 tablespoon turbinado sugar

14 whole cherries with stems attached, for garnish (optional)

Almond flour is made from ground blanched almonds and is available at natural and specialty foods stores such as Whole Foods. Almond meal often includes some almond skin and is coarser than almond flour. Either can be used in this recipe.

Preheat the oven to 400°F. Place paper liners in a muffin pan.

In a medium bowl, whisk together the flour, almond flour, baking powder, salt, and sugar. In another bowl, stir together the egg, milk, vanilla, and coconut oil or butter. Add the wet ingredients to the dry ingredients, stirring until just moistened. Fold in the chopped cherries. Fill the muffin cups three-quarters full. Sprinkle with turbinado sugar.

Bake for 15 minutes or until an inserted toothpick comes out clean. Cool slightly and top with one whole cherry, if desired.

Makes 12 to 14 muffins

Although I've placed this recipe in the brunch category, frittatas are on our regular dinner rotation. They're high in protein and can be made with almost any vegetables on hand. I love to include asparagus, cherry tomatoes, zucchini, mushrooms, and goat cheese, depending on what I have in the refrigerator or planter box. Here a dollop of tangy crème fraiche is the perfect complement to the potatoes and artichokes.

Potato and Artichoke Frittata

1 tablespoon extra-virgin olive oil

½ yellow onion, chopped

2 cloves garlic, minced

1 cup sliced potato, any color

Salt and freshly cracked pepper to taste

5 large eggs

¼ cup whole milk

¼ cup grated Parmesan cheese

1 cup jarred marinated artichoke hearts, drained

Crème fraiche, for garnish

Fresh herbs, such as Italian parsley, basil, or dill, for garnish

Preheat the oven to 450°F.

Heat the olive oil in a large ovenproof skillet over medium heat. Sauté the onion, garlic, and potato with a pinch of salt and pepper until tender, about 5 minutes. Meanwhile, whisk together the eggs, milk, and cheese. Pour the egg mixture over the potato mixture. Top with the artichokes. Reduce the heat to medium-low and cook until the eggs start to set, about 5 minutes. Transfer the pan to the oven and bake an additional 5 minutes or until the top of the frittata is set.

Cool slightly, remove from the pan, and cut into wedges. Garnish with crème fraiche and herbs.

Serves 4 to 6

Stratas are an easy way to get vegetables into breakfast. I particularly like dark leafy greens like spinach, kale, and chard, but any vegetables will work. The top of the strata gets beautifully browned and crisp, while the underneath is light and cheesy.

Swiss Chard Strata

1 tablespoon extra-virgin olive oil

5 cups chopped Swiss chard (about 1 large bunch)

6 large eggs

1 cup milk

1¼ cups shredded Italian cheese, such as mozzarella,
    Asiago, Parmesan, or a blend

½ teaspoon salt

¼ teaspoon freshly cracked pepper

1½ cups cubed day-old crusty French or Italian bread

¼ cup fresh basil leaves

Preheat the oven to 350°F. Coat a medium casserole dish or an 8-inch square baking dish with cooking spray.

Heat the olive oil in a large skillet over medium heat. Add the chard and a pinch of salt. Toss to coat. Cook until wilted, about 5 minutes. Transfer the chard to the casserole dish. In a medium bowl, whisk together the eggs, milk, cheese, salt, and pepper. Place the bread cubes on top of the chard and pour the egg mixture over the bread.

Bake for 50 minutes or until the eggs have set. Cool for 5 minutes. Garnish with basil.

Serves 6

I make the girls oatmeal for breakfast a few times per week. Natural oatmeal sweetened with agave syrup and topped with some milk and berries is a healthy way to start the day. On weekends I like to make oatmeal a little more fun by baking it with fruit and nuts. Strawberry rhubarb is one of my favorite combinations. Sprinkling the top with raw sugar adds a crunchy sweet crust to the soft, warm oatmeal.

Strawberry Rhubarb Baked Oatmeal

2 cups quick cooking or rolled oats (quick oats will
    produce a more cakelike texture)
1 teaspoon baking powder
¼ teaspoon salt
¼ cup sliced almonds, plus 1 tablespoon
2 large eggs
1 cup milk
½ cup agave syrup
2 tablespoons melted coconut oil
2 stalks rhubarb, cut into ¼-inch slices
1¼ cups sliced strawberries
1 tablespoon turbinado sugar

Preheat the oven to 350°F. Lightly coat a 9 × 13-inch baking dish with cooking spray.

In a medium bowl, stir together the oats, baking powder, salt, and ¼ cup almonds. In another medium bowl, whisk together the eggs, milk, agave syrup, and coconut oil. Pour the wet ingredients, rhubarb, and 1 cup of strawberries into the oat mixture and quickly stir until just combined. Pour the oatmeal into the baking dish and sprinkle the top with the remaining ¼ cup of strawberries and 1 tablespoon of sugar.

Bake for 40 to 50 minutes, or until bubbling and the edges have turned golden brown. Rolled oats will take slightly longer than quick oats. Cool for 5 to 10 minutes before serving. Serve in bowls with additional milk, if desired.

Serves 6

Kids love smoothies, and so do I. They are a tasty way to eat a large serving of fruit and are perfect for breakfast or snack time. Kefir is found next to the yogurt. It is high in probiotics, which give your immune system a great boost, and high in protein. This smoothie is packed with antioxidants and is sure to keep kids and mommies healthy. Keep a few bags of your favorite fruit in the freezer at all times and you will always be prepared to make your own smoothies.

Kefir Berry Power Smoothie

½ cup vanilla kefir

¼ cup pomegranate juice

1 cup frozen blueberries

1 cup frozen strawberries

Agave syrup to taste (optional)

Place all the ingredients in a blender and blend until smooth. Add agave syrup by the ½ teaspoonful to taste.

Serves 2

Not all blenders are the same. If your blender stops turning the smoothie ingredients, add more juice. Turn the blender off and stir with a spoon, but never put a spoon in a blender that is running.

This smoothie tastes like a milk shake, but without the ice cream.
I like it for a quick breakfast or an afternoon energy boost. Kids
like it because it's slightly chocolaty, but it really contains a very
small amount of chocolate.

Chocolate Almond Smoothie

½ cup milk
1 banana, sliced and frozen
¼ cup almond butter
1 tablespoon chocolate syrup
½ cup ice

Place all the ingredients in a blender and blend until
smooth.

Serves 2

Check the ingredients before assuming store-bought smoothies are health food. Many are made with several scoops of ice cream or sugar syrup, making them more like dessert.

for the meat lovers

Basil and Goat Cheese Stuffed Chicken Breasts with Peaches

Creamy Gnocchi with Chicken and Broccoli

Mom's Favorite Chicken Stroganoff

Herbs of Provence Pork Tenderloin with Strawberry Sauce

Lean and Juicy Turkey Burgers

Chicken Curry McCutcheon

A TIME FOR MEAT

For my first Mother's Day Phil gave me the best and worst present I could imagine. A new mom with a precious baby girl, I expected something sentimental or thoughtful, like a necklace or a pedicure. Instead, I was directed outside to find a big bulky barbecue grill. I looked at it, confused, and then back at my proudly grinning husband. "You want me to make you burgers? For Mother's Day?" I grumbled. I thought barbecuing was daddy territory.

Although not the typical Mother's Day gift, the barbecue is now one of my favorite and most used presents. During the warmer months I am especially thankful for my little outdoor cooking space. As the kids run through sprinklers giggling wildly, I revel in grilling fresh vegetables, pizzas, and even meats. Standing at the grill barefoot in my cotton sundress, feeling the heat radiate, and listening to the sizzle of the food on the hot grates, I am secretly pleased that my husband doesn't know how to use the grill. Outdoor entertaining, whether it's just our family or all of our friends, is so carefree and happy. Sitting on a picnic blanket on the lawn with the kids enjoying a juicy burger beats any restaurant experience, as far as I'm concerned. Barbecues bring friends and family together in a way that makes everyone feel at home. The distinctive smoky smell of an outdoor barbecue has been woven into my childhood memories of summer, and I'm sure it will be the same for my children.

Meat has a place in those memorable barbecues. Our family follows a mostly meatless diet, but I do have an appreciation for meat and believe it has a place. There are times when Phil, the girls, or I just crave a burger. Protein is important, and it is thought that animal proteins are better absorbed by our bodies than vegetable proteins. Both Phil and I are athletic and we have growing girls, so protein is something I have to take seriously. The moment I crossed the finish line at my last half marathon, all I could think about was a juicy burger. I don't feel guilty about that, as I know that listening to one's body is a good thing. Sometimes when I feel tired and know I am low on iron, I will opt for chicken breast or other meat. I avoid factory-farmed meat or animals treated with antibiotics or hormones by shopping at stores that label their products as "grass fed," "organic," and "free range," because I care about the animals and keeping hormones and antibiotics out of our diets.

The recipes in this chapter are lighter than average meat dishes. These recipes are the solution for families with the common conundrum in which some want meat and others prefer a light and healthy meal. My Lean and Juicy Turkey Burgers (page 278), for example, satisfy the desire for a hearty and comforting burger, but are low-fat.

Only a small percentage of the population is vegetarian, and many people expect meat for dinner. At the same time, many are trying to cut down on meat, whether it's for health, environmental, or ethical reasons. In my day-to-day life I usually don't consume any meat other than fish. If I'm having a dinner party for a large number of meat lovers, however, I might serve a healthy, easy, and elegant chicken dish like Chicken Curry McCutcheon (page 282).

For summertime barbecues, feeding meat-loving family and friends, and responding to our bodies' need for high-quality protein, meat can be a nourishing and delicious part of a healthy lifestyle. Family barbecues don't have to mean processed hot dogs and beef cheeseburgers, and chicken doesn't have to be fried and fatty to be comfort food. This chapter gives you an instant repertoire of effortlessly elegant wholesome recipes to feed the carnivores in your life.

This summery chicken dish is one of my favorites. The bright flavors of peaches, white wine, basil, and tangy goat cheese make skinless chicken breast more fun and flavorful than usual. The couscous only takes 5 minutes to make and soaks up all the flavorful juices of the sauce.

Basil and Goat Cheese Stuffed Chicken Breasts with Peaches

2 tablespoons unsalted butter

1¼ cups dry white wine

½ cup chicken stock

1 sprig fresh thyme

1 teaspoon honey

1 peach, pitted and cut into half-slices

Salt and freshly cracked pepper to taste

2 large chicken breasts (6 to 8 ounces each)

4 ounces goat cheese

¼ cup chopped fresh basil, plus more for garnish

2 tablespoons extra-virgin olive oil

1 cup uncooked couscous

To make the peach sauce, melt the butter in a small saucepan over medium heat until it starts to turn golden brown. Add the wine, stock, thyme, and honey, and simmer for 20 minutes. Stir in the peaches and simmer 5 minutes longer. Remove the thyme sprig. Season with salt and pepper, if desired.

Place the chicken breasts between two sheets of wax paper and pound to the thickness of ¼ inch with a meat mallet or a rolling pin. Season the chicken with salt and pepper. Stir together the goat cheese and the ¼ cup basil. Divide in half. Spread a log of cheese lengthwise down the center of each of the chicken breasts and roll the chicken lengthwise over the cheese. Secure with kitchen twine or toothpicks. Heat the olive oil in a large frying or sauté pan over medium-high heat. Brown the chicken on all sides until cooked through.

While chicken is cooking, cook the couscous according to package instructions.

Divide the couscous among four plates. Slice each chicken roll in half and place a half on top of the couscous on each plate. Spoon the peach sauce over the top. Garnish with fresh basil.

Serves 4

Creamy Gnocchi with Chicken and Broccoli

17 ounces potato gnocchi

2½ cups broccoli florets

1 cup milk

1 clove garlic, minced

4 ounces mascarpone cheese

½ cup grated Parmesan cheese

1 cup shredded cooked chicken breast

Salt and freshly cracked pepper to taste

¼ cup fresh basil, torn

Bring a large pot of salted water to a boil. Place the gnocchi in the boiling water. When the gnocchi rise to the surface after about 3 minutes, add the broccoli and continue to cook for 2 minutes. Remove from the heat and promptly drain and rinse with cool water. In the same pot over medium heat, bring the milk and garlic to a simmer. Stir in the mascarpone and Parmesan until combined. Add the chicken, gnocchi, and broccoli and toss together. Season to taste with salt and pepper and pour into a serving dish. Sprinkle with basil.

Serves 4

Almost every year since I was a little girl my mom has asked my dad to make Chicken Stroganoff on her birthday. Dad has spent years perfecting his recipe, and I'm happy to be able to share it with you. There are strong flavors here, but they are mellowed by the pasta and creamy sauce. My brother and I loved it even as kids, and my girls love it now.

Mom's Favorite Chicken Stroganoff

Lighten up! Crème fraiche gives this dish a silky creaminess. If you are making this more often than just on special occasions and want to significantly reduce the fat content, replace the crème fraiche with low-fat plain Greek yogurt. Once the yogurt is added, however, make sure the sauce gently simmers, but never boils, or it may curdle.

4 medium-size chicken breasts (6 ounces each)

2 cups whole cremini mushrooms

2¼ cups dry sherry

2 tablespoons olive oil

1 medium yellow onion, sliced

1 clove garlic, crushed

¼ cup chicken stock

2 cups crème fraiche

2 tablespoons finely chopped fresh basil, plus 12 whole
    basil leaves for garnish

10 ounces extra-wide egg noodles, such as No Yolks

½ cup marinated sun-dried tomatoes, julienned

Place the chicken, mushrooms, and 2 cups of the sherry in a large bowl. Cover and marinate overnight. Drain the chicken and mushrooms and discard sherry liquid.

Heat the olive oil in a large skillet over medium-high heat. Add the chicken to the skillet and cook until nicely browned, about 5 minutes. Reduce heat to low and cook for an additional 15 minutes. Remove the chicken from the pan, transfer to a cutting board, and cut the chicken into ½-inch-thick slices.

Place the diced onion in the skillet and sauté for 4 minutes over medium-high heat. Add the marinated mushrooms and garlic to the skillet and continue to sauté over low heat for 4 minutes more. Add the chicken stock to the onions and mushrooms. Transfer the sliced chicken back into the skillet. Stir in the remaining ¼ cup sherry. Simmer 5 minutes, until the sauce has reduced slightly. Stir in the crème fraiche and chopped basil. Season to taste with salt and pepper. Simmer over low heat.

Cook the noodles in a large pot of salted water according to package directions. Drain and lightly drizzle with olive oil to prevent the noodles from sticking together.

Place a bed of noodles on each plate. Place the chicken and sauce mixture on top of noodles and top with sun-dried tomatoes. Garnish with whole or torn fresh basil leaves.

Serves 6

Herbs of Provence is my favorite dried herb blend. A mixture of thyme, savory, lavender, fennel, and sometimes other herbs, herbs of Provence makes a flavorful seasoning in one step. I add it to sauces and rub it on meat.

Herbs of Provence Pork Tenderloin with Strawberry Sauce

2 tablespoons extra-virgin olive oil

1 (1¼-pound) pork tenderloin

1 tablespoon herbs of Provence

Salt and freshly cracked pepper

2 tablespoons unsalted butter

2 sprigs fresh rosemary, plus more for garnish

2 sprigs fresh thyme, plus more for garnish

1 cup dry white wine

½ cup chicken broth

1 cup chopped strawberries, plus 2 to 3 halved
     strawberries, for garnish

1 teaspoon balsamic vinegar

My favorite herbs of Provence mix is made in France and comes in a small clay pot. Find it at Williams-Sonoma, Sur la Table, and some grocery stores.

Preheat the oven to 350°F.

Heat the olive oil over medium-high heat in a cast-iron skillet. Rub the herbs, ¼ teaspoon salt, and a pinch of pepper into the pork tenderloin. Brown the tenderloin on all sides. Transfer to a baking dish and place in the oven. Bake until a thermometer reads 145°F, about 25 minutes. Let rest for 15 minutes, then cut into 1-inch slices.

Meanwhile, in a small saucepan melt the butter over medium heat until it starts to turn golden brown. Add the rosemary, thyme, wine, broth, and strawberries. Reduce the heat to medium-low and simmer for 30 minutes.

Stir in the balsamic vinegar and remove from the heat. Season to taste with salt and pepper. Serve warm with the pork tenderloin. Garnish with rosemary, thyme, and fresh strawberries, if desired.

Serves 4

White turkey meat is a healthy alternative to beef, but often results in dry burgers. The secret ingredient to keeping these burgers moist is low-fat cottage cheese. The curds melt, creating an incredibly juicy burger even with 99 percent fat-free meat. Fresh ginger and cilantro infuse the patties with sophisticated flavor, making this recipe a winner with both adults and kids.

Lean and Juicy Turkey Burgers

1¼ pounds ground turkey breast

2 teaspoons minced ginger

¼ cup low-fat cottage cheese

½ cup fresh cilantro, chopped

¼ cup teriyaki sauce, plus more for serving

6 medium-size rolls, halved

6 butter lettuce leaves

1 large tomato, thinly sliced

Ketchup (optional)

In a large bowl, stir together the turkey, ginger, cottage cheese, cilantro, and ¼ cup teriyaki sauce until just combined. Lightly coat your hands with cooking spray and form the meat into 6 patties. Lightly coat the grill with cooking spray and heat to medium-high. Cook patties, covered, until dark grill marks can be seen, about 5 minutes. Flip and continue cooking until completely cooked through and the internal temperature has reached 165°F, about 5 minutes longer.

Place the rolls, cut side down, on the hot grill for 2 minutes until toasted. Place 1 piece of lettuce on the bottom piece of each roll. Top with the patties, tomato slices, and the top halves of the rolls. Serve with ketchup or additional teriyaki sauce.

Serves 6

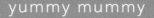

LIFE TIP

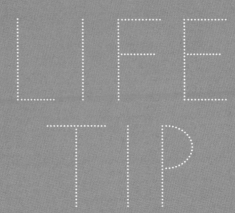

My favorite way to entertain is with laidback barbecues and picnics. Serve Lean and Juicy Turkey Burgers (page 278) with vegetables brushed with olive oil, sprinkled with salt and pepper, and grilled right along with the patties during the last 4 minutes of cooking. Prepare a make-ahead dessert like Strawberry Lemonade Tiramisu (page 214) the night before.

I like to keep the ingredients for a party on hand for mommy happy-hour play dates and backyard barbecues, and that includes the beverages. Fun drinks make any celebration more festive, and a glass of cold white sangria with colorful fruit floating in it is my favorite party drink. I love peach sangria, but you can use just about any fruit and juice you have on hand.

Peach White Sangria
1 bottle white wine
1 bottle sparkling white wine
3 cups peach juice
2 peaches, pitted and sliced
2 oranges, sliced
1 cup raspberries
½ cup fresh mint leaves

Pour all the ingredients into a large pitcher, stir, and serve cold.

Serves 8 to 10

This is a very old "secret" family recipe created by my great-grandmother Val and passed down to my grandmother Tai Tai, my mother, and me. Every Sunday in Hong Kong Tai Tai would get together for lunch with her group of six couples. She often served this curry for her friends to eat outside while they chatted and sipped shandies. This is a great recipe to feed a crowd—simply double the recipe below. The toppings served in bowls are what makes this recipe extra special, fun, and tasty. They add a variety of flavors, textures, and colors. Tai Tai served this curry very spicy. I have adapted this recipe so that, although it is very flavorful, it is not too spicy for kids.

Chicken Curry McCutcheon

Curry paste can be found in the Asian section of many grocery stores, including Whole Foods.

3 tablespoons olive oil, plus more as needed

2 large sweet yellow onions, chopped

2 cloves garlic, minced

2 teaspoons crushed or minced fresh ginger

2½ pounds boneless skinless chicken breasts, cut into
    bite-size pieces

1 teaspoon salt

½ teaspoon freshly cracked pepper

1 tablespoon curry paste

¼ cup tomato paste

2 cups chicken broth

1 small apple, peeled, cored, and chopped

Juice of 1 lemon

2 tablespoons coconut milk

6 cups cooked jasmine rice

1 cup lightly toasted flaked unsweetened coconut

1 cup mango or apple chutney

1 cup sliced bananas

1 cup chopped peanuts

1 cup raisins

1 cup sliced green onions

1 cup chopped hothouse or Persian cucumber

Heat the olive oil in a large frying pan over medium-high heat. Add the onion and sauté until starting to brown, about 10 minutes. Add the garlic and ginger, and sauté 1 minute longer. Transfer the onion, garlic, and ginger to a large stockpot, while leaving the oil in the frying pan.

Add the chicken pieces to the frying pan and season with salt and pepper. Brown chicken on all sides, about 5 minutes. Transfer the chicken to the stockpot with a slotted spoon, leaving any remaining oil in the pan (or add a bit more oil if necessary).

Reduce the heat to low and sauté the curry paste in the oil for 10 minutes. Add the tomato paste and sauté for another 10 minutes. Add the broth to the pan and boil the mixture for 5 minutes. Pour the sauce from frying pan into the stockpot. Add the apple and lemon juice to the stockpot and simmer over low heat for 20 minutes. Stir in the coconut milk just before serving.

Serve over rice, and place the coconut, chutney, bananas, peanuts, raisins, green onions, and cucumber in individual bowls to offer as toppings.

Serves 4 to 6

original yummy mummy

One afternoon Tai Tai, my mom, Aunt Ginny, and I were chatting
over quiche and shandy cocktails when I asked Tai Tai to share
her wisdom and tips for a happy family. She encouraged me to
have my husband spend some time enjoying hobbies of his own.
She said that sending fathers off for an hour of golf with their own
friends on the weekends or after work is a great idea. Don't tell him I
said so, but I've noticed my husband is in a much better mood after going on a half-
hour bike ride or playing tennis after work.

My girlfriends and I have often remarked that at the end of the day we are often
so exhausted that when our husbands get home from work, all we want to do is say,
"Here—take the kids! It's your turn!" We all know that we moms need occasional time
to ourselves, and I think what Tai Tai was trying to say is that it's good to remember
that dads need that time too—even when we feel like it is "their turn."

While daddy goes surfing or golfing or meets a friend for happy hour, pour yourself a cold glass of Tai Tai's Shandy Cocktail.

Tai Tai's Shandy Cocktail

2 beers
1 ginger beer or ginger ale
1 lemon, cut into wedges

Pour beer and ginger beer into a large pitcher and gently stir to combine. Serve over ice and garnish glasses with lemon wedges.

Serves 4

Soon after having my first baby I noticed a beautiful chalkboard calendar in my girl-friend Sarah's kitchen. Each night had a planned dinner written in, except for Saturday, which was usually reserved for a date night out. I followed Sarah's example and realized that having a weekly plan for dinner made my life much easier. Taking a few minutes each week to write down the week's dinner menus saves time and stress each night and makes grocery shopping easier.

To follow are mostly meatless weekly menu ideas for each season. Shopping lists include the ingredients you will need in addition to basic pantry staples (see page 303 for a list of pantry staples). Foods that perish quickly like fish or meat are best served the day they are bought, which is the reason the seafood recipes are on Sunday.

SPRING

Sunday: Make-Ahead Tilapia and Asparagus Baked in Parchment (page 182)

Monday: Rice Noodles Primavera with Tofu and Peanut Sauce (page 148)

Tuesday: Lentil Stuffed Portobello Mushrooms (page 140)

Wednesday: Veggie Cobb Salad (page 86)

Thursday: Mom's Best Quiche (page 106)

Friday: Veggie Tortilla Soup with Quinoa (page 60)

Saturday: Fiesta Burritos (page 113)

Shopping List

Produce
2 small bunches asparagus
3 yellow onions
8 carrots
3 stalks celery
2 zucchini
1 cup sugar snap peas
4 large portobello mushrooms (or 8 or
    more smaller portobellos)
1 cup sliced cremini mushrooms
2 large tomatoes
1 cup cherry tomatoes
5 avocados
1 leek

1 red bell pepper
1 yellow bell pepper
2 lemons
2 limes
8 ounces romaine lettuce

Fresh Herbs and Spices
1 small bunch green onions
1 large bunch cilantro
1 small piece ginger
1 small bunch oregano
1 small bunch thyme

Seafood
1 pound tilapia fillets

Refrigerator
7 ounces baked tofu

Cheese and Dairy
Grated Parmesan cheese
2 ounces Jarlsberg cheese
2 ounces Gruyère cheese
½ cup crumbled blue cheese
½ cup grated cheddar cheese
½ cup crumbled queso fresco or other

Mexican cheese
½ cup sour cream
½ cup heavy cream

Pantry
Peanut oil
Soy sauce
Ground cumin
Ground coriander
10 ounces rice noodles
¼ cup peanuts
1 cup croutons

Bread
1 large package corn or flour tortillas (either
    can be used for both the Veggie Tortilla
    Soup with Quinoa and the Fiesta Burritos)

SUMMER

Sunday: Macadamia-Crusted Mahi Mahi with Mango Couscous (page 160)

Monday: Mandarin Tofu Stir Fry (page 142)

Tuesday: Basil and Goat Cheese Stuffed Chicken Breasts with Peaches (page 270)

Wednesday: Grilled Shrimp and Corn Salad (page 94)

Thursday: Black Bean Burgers with Mango-Avocado Salsa (page 108)

Friday: Easy Greens and Goat Cheese Lasagna (page 138)

Saturday: Summer Squash Rainbow Pizza (page 122)

Shopping List

Produce
2 carrots
4 ounces broccolini
1 baby bok choy
1 red bell pepper
1 red onion
1 cup sugar snap peas

1 peach
1 medium mango
1 leek
1 bunch asparagus
2 zucchini
1 yellow squash
5 ounces fresh baby spinach

2 heads romaine lettuce
1 small head green leaf lettuce
4 limes
3 ears corn
½ cup cherry tomatoes
2 Roma tomatoes
2 avocados
1 small shallot
1 pomegranate (optional)

Fresh Herbs and Spices

1 large bunch cilantro
1 bunch basil
1 small bunch thyme
1 small piece ginger

Seafood

4 (6-ounce) mahi mahi fillets
1 pound large peeled, deveined shrimp

Poultry

2 large chicken breasts (6 to 8 ounces each)

Refrigerator

Orange juice
8 ounces extra-firm tofu
14-ounce container fresh mango salsa
4 ounces pesto
1 (16-ounce) prepared pizza dough

Cheese and Dairy

9 ounces goat cheese
3 ounces shredded Monterey Jack cheese
15 ounces ricotta cheese
4 ounces shredded Italian cheese, such as
    mozzarella, Parmesan, Asiago, or a blend
1 ounce feta cheese

Pantry

1 cup macadamia nuts
½ cup flaked coconut
Soy sauce
Sesame oil
1 (11-ounce) can mandarin oranges
1 bag jasmine rice
15 ounces couscous
Ground cumin
Dried oregano
Plain breadcrumbs
1 package fresh or no-boil lasagna noodles

Bread

1 small package pita bread pockets

Beverages

1 bottle dry white wine

FALL

Sunday: Crispy Baked "Fish and Chips" (page 172)
Monday: Veggie-Loaded Chili (page 62)
Tuesday: Creamy Gnocchi with Chicken and Broccoli (page 273)
Wednesday: Grilled Tilapia Gyros (page 174)
Thursday: Baked Spaghetti Squash and "Meatballs" (page 135)
Friday: Honey-Curry Glazed Vegetables and Garbanzos (page 124)
Saturday: Dad's Garlic Ricotta Calzone (page 120)

Shopping List

Produce
3 russet potatoes
1 yellow onion
7 carrots
2 stalks celery
1 sweet potato
1 red bell pepper
1 small head broccoli
1 lemon
2 Persian cucumbers
1 medium tomato
1 avocado
½ cup fresh baby spinach
1 large spaghetti squash
1 large head cauliflower

Fresh Herbs and Spices
1 bunch parsley
1 bunch cilantro
1 small bunch green onions
2 large bunches basil
1 small bunch dill

Seafood
1 pound tilapia or halibut fillets
1 pound tilapia fillets (I recommend buying fresh fish no more than one day before you plan to use it.)

Poultry
1 cup shredded cooked chicken breast

Refrigerator
2 cups marinara or spaghetti sauce
1 (16-ounce) prepared pizza dough or yeast to make homemade dough

Cheese and Dairy
1 (8-ounce) container plain low-fat Greek yogurt
1 (8-ounce) container sour cream
4 ounces mascarpone cheese

2 cups ricotta cheese
2 cups grated Parmesan cheese
½ cup shredded mozzarella cheese
2 cups grated Asiago cheese

Pantry
1 package panko breadcrumbs
Chili powder
Cumin
Curry powder
1 small can or tube tomato paste

17 ounces potato gnocchi
¼ cup pepitas (pumpkin seeds)
¼ cup pine nuts

Bread
1 (approximately 11-ounce) package flat
    bread

Freezer
16 ounces meatless meatballs
1 small package spinach

WINTER

Sunday: 15-Minute Mascarpone Fettuccine with Broiled Salmon (page 162)

Monday: Green Enchiladas (page 150)

Tuesday: Mom's Favorite Chicken Stroganoff (page 274)

Wednesday: Spaghetti with Roasted Butternut Squash, Peas, and Sage Pesto (page 116)

Thursday: Southwestern Quinoa Stuffed Peppers (page 130)

Friday: Cauliflower Mac and Cheese (page 110)

Saturday: Lentil Soup (page 50)

Shopping List

Produce
1 cup microgreens
10 ounces fresh baby spinach
3½ cups sliced cremini mushrooms
2 medium yellow onions
1 medium butternut squash
1 package frozen or fresh peas
4 bell peppers, any color
1 ear corn
1 cup cherry tomatoes

3 cups cauliflower florets
2 carrots
2 stalks celery
1 large russet potato
1 avocado
1 lime

Fresh Herbs and Spices
1 small bunch parsley
2 bunches cilantro

2 bunches basil
1 bunch sage

Seafood
¾ pound wild salmon

Poultry
4 medium-size chicken breasts (6 ounces each)

Refrigerator
1 small package extra-firm tofu

Cheese and Dairy
8 ounces whole milk
½ cup half and half
1½ cups grated Parmesan cheese
¼ cup shaved Parmesan cheese
¼ cup shredded Monterey Jack cheese
1½ cups shredded sharp cheddar cheese
1 cup shredded Mexican cheese, Monterey Jack, cheddar, Colby, or a blend

6 ounces mascarpone cheese
2 ounces goat cheese
2 cups crème fraiche or low-fat plain Greek yogurt

Pantry
8 ounces fresh or dried fettuccine
16 ounces mild tomatillo green salsa
10 ounces extra-wide egg noodles, such as No Yolks
1 small jar marinated julienne-cut sun-dried tomatoes
Whole nutmeg
¾ cup pine nuts
Panko breadcrumbs

Bread
1 package of at least 6 (9-inch) flour or brown-rice tortillas

Beverages
1 bottle dry sherry

SPRING: PICNIC DINNER

In the spring and summer, when the days are long, our friends like to gather at the park for dinner. Eating a light dinner outdoors is refreshing, and the kids love kicking balls around with their friends. We bring easy picnic dinners and a bottle of wine or sparkling lemonade to share. Don't forget the plates and napkins!

Bottles of favorite sparkling lemonade and white wine
Effortless Edamame-Basil Hummus Dip (page 26)
Baked pita chips
Grilled Shrimp and Corn Salad (page 94)
Peanut Butter and Jelly Granola Bars (page 252)

SUMMER: BIRTHDAY PARTY

Summer birthday parties are the perfect excuse for kids to play past naptime while friends and family relax on the patio. Stick to simple mostly make-ahead recipes so that you can spend the party celebrating instead of cooking. Prepare the sangria in the morning and the ice cream pies a day or two in advance. Lean and Juicy Turkey Burgers are a healthy and tasty alternative to traditional barbecued birthday hamburgers.

Peach White Sangria (page 280)
Carrot and celery sticks
Lean and Juicy Turkey Burgers (page 278)
Mini Ice Cream Pies (page 190), with several types of sprinkles set out for topping

FALL: POST–SOCCER GAME GET-TOGETHER

When the air turns brisk in the fall, we crave warm comforting foods. After a busy day of fun, the last thing you want is to be scrambling to make dinner for a hungry crowd. Choose recipes like these, which can be prepared ahead of time for a stress-free party. Chili is an easy recipe to feed a large group and is always a crowd-pleaser. Make it early in the day and keep it warm in a slow cooker or reheat it over medium-low heat on the stove. Make the trifle the night before the party. To simplify this menu even more, use a mix to make corn muffins early in the morning in place of the sandwiches.

Tai Tai's Shandy Cocktail (page 285)
Mini Apple Cheddar Grilled Cheese Sandwiches (page 10)
Veggie-Loaded Chili (page 62)
Pumpkin and Chocolate Mousse Trifle (page 224)

WINTER: HOLIDAY CELEBRATION

During the holidays it's fun to have friends and family over and to celebrate with appetizers in an open-house setting. I love to turn on holiday music, set out festive finger foods, and let the kids decorate gingerbread cookies while the parents chat. These hors d'oeuvres are perfect for a happy-hour celebration. To make it more of a dinner, set out a store-bought ham with honey mustard or shrimp cocktails. Prepare the cookie dough and sugared cranberries one day in advance so that there is little work right before the party.

Store-bought apple cider
Champagne
Mixed nuts
Pear, Humboldt Fog Cheese, and Honey Crisps (page 39)
Sparkling Cranberry and Brie Bites (page 18)
Raspberry Endives with Candied Pecans (page 43)
Chocolate Hazelnut Shortbread (page 207)

Tips for Getting Kids to Eat and Enjoy Vegetables

When I hear parents gripe that their children "won't eat veggies," I always wonder why this is. Is there an innate preference for mac and cheese, cheese crackers, and other white or orange processed foods? I once heard a true story of a three-year-old Italian boy visiting his grandmother here in America. The grandmother provided animal-shaped cheese crackers and the little boy asked in disbelief, "This is food?" Accustomed to being served risotto with fresh vegetables for snack time at preschool, he found the bright orange snack quite novel.

In health-conscious Santa Barbara, seeing children eat tomatoes like apples and get excited about baby bell peppers is not an uncommon sight. The Santa Barbara farmers' markets, of which there are eight per week, are bustling with happy children with chins dripping with strawberry juice. Paying attention to my students' and now my own kids' and their friends' eating habits, I have noticed behaviors that make kids more likely to eat and enjoy their vegetables.

Bring kids to the farmers' market.

Get excited about the colors and produce that changes with the seasons at the market. Your kids will get excited too and will be much more likely to try new vegetables.

Subscribe to a local CSA and have a produce box delivered weekly.

If getting to the farmers' market doesn't fit into your schedule, try a weekly or biweekly produce box delivered from a local farm or CSA (Community Supported Agriculture). Every Thursday my kids feel as though they are getting a present delivered and eagerly dive into our produce box. Again, when they get excited about exploring the food, they are more likely to enjoy it.

Cook with your kids.

Most kids love to cook as much as they love to paint or make mud pies in the backyard. Allowing them to help with meal preparation gives kids a sense of pride in what they have made.

Let your kids choose vegetables at a nursery and help them plant a backyard garden.

Homegrown sugar snap peas and cherry tomatoes off the vine taste better and are certainly more exciting for children than vegetables in a carton at the supermarket.

Don't assume kids are averse to any foods.

In college I babysat the one-year-old of a talented restaurant chef. The toddler refused to eat the pasta and vegetables his mother asked me to make. Later his mom explained that I needed to season the dish the way I would like it, not the bland way I expected babies to eat. This distinction made sense to me and was something I remembered when I had babies of my own. Soon after my kids started eating solids, they were getting the flavors of onions, garlic, herbs, and vegetables. Instead of steaming and pureeing vegetables or giving jars of baby food, I gave very soft pieces of avocado, roasted sweet potato fries, and diced vegetables that had been cooked in soups. Don't be afraid to give children flavorful foods.

Almost every restaurant kids' menu I come across is lacking vegetables other than French fries. There is an expectation that kids don't like vegetables. That expectation is the very reason kids don't (or think they don't) like vegetables. Both of my kids ask for tomato, lettuce, and grilled onions on their hamburgers when we are out at a beachside restaurant. They get strange looks from other adults, but there is no reason these sweet, mild ingredients should be offensive to a child's palate.

Put vegetables in everything.

Most of my dinners are one-dish meals that include lots of vegetables, making them, in a sense, unavoidable. Instead of a pile of steamed vegetables served on the side, they are the main focus of the dinner. Vegetables intertwined with pasta, baked in a casserole, or bulking up a soup seem less daunting to kids. With dinners like these, kids will quickly get used to eating vegetables.

Don't offer alternatives at dinnertime.

I don't have the time or energy to make separate dinners for the kids, so I never have. Knowing only one dinner will be made, they don't think to ask for something else. Making separate "kid dinners" can be a difficult habit to break, but once kids realize mom is not getting up from the dinner table once dinner is served, they will stop asking. Kids will not starve if you don't make what they request.

No snacks after four thirty in the afternoon.

This is something I learned from my mom. We never ate snacks after four thirty and we were always hungry and ready to eat at six. It is hard to say no to hungry children in the late afternoon, but it's also not fair to expect children who are not hungry to clean their plates. Children will quickly adapt to the new routine and eat their healthy dinners.

Having a well-stocked pantry makes cooking faster and easier. Loading up on fresh produce once or twice a week and keeping these staples on hand means that trips to the grocery store are limited and there is always something quick and healthy to prepare.

Pantry

All-purpose flour

Whole-wheat flour

Baking powder

Baking soda

Granulated sugar

Brown sugar

Vanilla extract

Quinoa

Brown rice

Rolled oats

Pasta (spaghetti, medium shapes such as penne and bowties, and small ones such as orzo and macaroni)

Lentils

Canned beans (kidney, black, cannellini, garbanzo)

Boxed or canned chopped or crushed tomatoes (Pomi is my favorite brand)

Vegetable or chicken broth

Peanut butter

Dijon mustard

Onion

Garlic

Wholesome Sweeteners

Agave syrup

Turbinado sugar

Honey

Maple syrup

Wholesome Fats

Coconut oil

Extra-virgin olive oil

Vegetable oil

By the Stove

Finishing salts such as fleur de sel, pink salt, and black salt

Kosher salt

Peppermill with whole peppercorns

Herbs of Provence

Refrigerator

Carrots

Celery

Baby spinach or mixed green baby lettuces

Plain low-fat Greek yogurt

Cheese

Eggs

Unsalted butter

Milk (1 or 2 percent)

Freezer

Puff pastry

Prepared piecrust (homemade or all-butter store-bought)

Garlic and herb cubes (such as Dorot brand, available at Trader Joe's, Whole Foods, and other grocery stores)

Peeled, deveined shrimp (use within three months)

Edamame

Spinach

Berries

Nuts (Once opened, nuts quickly go rancid. Keeping them in the freezer ensures there will always be fresh nuts available.)

INDEX

SCAN THIS CODE
WITH YOUR SMARTPHONE TO BE LINKED TO THE BONUS MATERIALS FOR

THE YUMMY MUMMY KITCHEN

on the Elixir mobile website,
where you can also find information about other
healthy living books and related materials

YOU CAN ALSO TEXT
MUMMY to READIT (732348)

to be sent a link to the Elixir mobile website.

 Facebook.com/elixirliving   Twitter.com/elixirliving